HIKING
DOLOMITES

The Complete Trekking Guide with Maps — Day Hikes, Rifugi Treks & Alta Via Routes from Cortina, Val Gardena, Ortisei, Tre Cime & Beyond

LIAM OMAR

Copyright © 2025 by Liam Omar

All rights reserved

No part of this publication may be reproduced, distributed, or transmitted in any form or by any means, including photocopying, recording, or other electronic or mechanical methods, without the prior written permission of the publisher, except in the case of brief quotations embodied in critical reviews and certain other noncommercial uses permitted by copyright law.

CONTENTS

INTRODUCTION — 10

GET ORIENTED — 18
Location and Geography — 18
The Parks — 20
Valleys and Mountain Hubs — 22
Language — 25
When to Visit — 27
Types of Hiking Experiences — 32

PLANNING YOUR TRIP — 37
Recommended Hiking Routes — 38
Best Home Bases by Interest — 42
How to Combine Regions without Excessive Travel — 44
Lodging Options in the Dolomites — 46
How to Book Rifugi (and When Do They Open) — 48

GETTING THERE AND AROUND — 51

Closest Airports	52
Train Connections and Mountain Transfers	55
Car Rental Tips: Freedom and Responsibility	56
Cable Cars and Funivia	57
Public Transport vs. Rental Car	59
Dolomiti Mobility Cards: Comfort in Your Pocket	61

TOP HIKING DESTINATIONS — 66

Tre Cime di Lavaredo & Surroundings	66
Alta Via 1	74
Alta Via 2	82
Seceda & Odle Group (Val Gardena)	88
Seiser Alm (Alpe di Siusi)	95
Sassolungo and Sassopiatto	103
Cinque Torri & Lagazuoi	111
Rosengarten/Catinaccio Group	120
Pale di San Martino	128
Fanes-Sennes-Braies Natural Park	137
Lago di Braies and Extension Hikes	145

Tofane Group (Cortina d'Ampezzo Area)	153
Monte Pelmo and Civetta (Dolomiti Bellunesi)	162

LOCAL CULTURE ALONG THE TRAILS — 173

Ladin Heritage and Villages	174
Alpine Cuisine to Savor Following the Hike	175
Alpine Dairies (Malgas) and Cheese Tasting	176
Local Legends and WWI Remnants	178

PRACTICAL TIPS AND ADVICE — 182

Trail Safety and Essentials	183
Trailhead Parking and Regulations	185
Crowds and How to Avoid Them	186
Travel Insurance	187
Budgeting	188
Language Tips for Hikers	189

Introduction

There's a moment in the Dolomites that remains with you—when the light turns the cliffs to flame, when silence envelopes a high-altitude rifugio, and jagged limestone blades slice into an ocean of blue. It's not about performance or exaggeration. It is the nature of these mountains.

The Dolomites, designated a UNESCO World Heritage Site for "their monumental and exceptional beauty," are more than just mountains; they are drama fashioned from time. A remarkable combination of vertical limestone cathedrals, glacier-carved valleys, and high-alpine pastures dotted with houses and chapels that appear to have been softly dropped from heaven. A place where geology, history, culture, and adventure meet in a cinematic way.

One does not simply hike through the Dolomites. The routes wind through former conflict zones and whispering pine forests, across scree slopes where marmots chirp warnings, and through meadows brimming with gentians, arnica, and wild thyme. The routes are well-worn, but never tame. What begins as a hike frequently transforms into something altogether different—part pilgrimage, part performance, and part interaction with nature.

Why the Mountains Keep Calling

Hiking opportunities abound. Few provide this. The Dolomites are remarkable for their concentrated brilliance—dozens of legendary routes, all in close proximity, yet each valley has its own accent, food, and architectural style. It represents the alpine variation in its most layered and graceful form.

- The Peaks: Unlike the snow-covered silhouettes of the Alps further west, the Dolomites rise in vertical slabs, needles, and towers. Their distinctive pale tint, which stems from old coral reef beginnings, takes on surreal hues at dawn and sunset, when enrosadira (the legendary alpenglow) paints the rock scarlet and rose.

- The Dolomite paths, which are waymarked by the Italian Alpine Club (CAI), are among the best-maintained in Europe. Whether it's a morning loop through Alpe di Siusi's wide flower-filled meadows or a multi-day journey over the high Alta Via roads, every path leads somewhere wild, fabled, or serene.
- The Rifugi is unique in that it mixes difficult mountain hiking with high-altitude comfort. Rifugi dot the mountains like alpine lighthouses, serving warm pasta, strudel, and local wines at elevations of 2,500 meters. After a long day of walking, stepping into dry socks alongside a wooden table engraved with names and stories from the past... Few things compare.
- History: These mountains recall. The Dolomites were a frontline during World War I, and vestiges remain: tunnels blasted through rock faces, rusted helmets beside wildflowers, and stone trenches above the tree line. History does not feel remote here; it is there with every step.
- The Culture: Germanic accuracy, Italian warmth, and Ladin heritage combine in unexpected

harmony. One walk may go past wooden Tyrolean farmhouses, the next to a chapel with frescoes older than most countries. Local shepherds speak three languages, and meals feature both Schlutzkrapfen and gnocchi. It's not fusion; it's a deep-rooted coexistence.

Hiking Season at a Glance

The hiking season peaks between late June and early October. This window provides the most accessible circumstances, with cable cars functioning, rifugi open, and snow-free trails above 2,000 meters. Alpine flora blooms in July and August, and the days are long. September covers the larches in gold, a quieter, sharper moment as the season begins to fade.

- Wildflowers are at their height from late June until mid-July. Trails are uncrowded. Snow may remain on high passes, but lower routes bloom in full color.
- High season: mid-July to late August. Rifugi are bustling, cableways are fully operational, and the valleys are filled with the clink of trekking poles and laughter. Book in advance—this is when the Dolomites come alive.
- September until early October: Autumn magic. Crisp air, golden trees, and calmer pathways. Some

rifugi begin to close in late September, while the lower and mid-altitude pathways remain open and beautiful.

What matters the most? Hike smartly. Weather changes quickly at altitude. Even in clear blue skies, carry a shell. And always, always allow for slowness. The Dolomites reward those who linger.

A Landscape Etched in Memory

Atop a short mountain above Val Gardena, clouds slip below boot height. To the west, the Sassolungo group rises like an ancient castle. Cowbells reverberate faintly from below, transported by updrafts. The moment extends. The world below shrinks. Nothing here asks to be earned, but everything feels like a reward.

This is what it is about. Not only the peaks, but what happens in between.

The Dolomites provide an incredible variety of terrains, each a universe unto itself:

- Odle Group's spiny pinnacles, sharp as shark teeth.
- The spectacular sweep of the Alpe di Siusi, with its green openness framed by giants
- Pale di San Martino's stony plateaus are empty like the moon.
- The battle-scarred trails of Cinque Torri and Lagazuoi are still haunted by the ghosts of war.
- Tre Cime di Lavaredo is postcard-perfect, towering guard over everything.

Despite this wonder, the pattern remains—the trail underfoot, the pause to breathe, the way light bends over stone. The Dolomites are not simply seen. They are sensed.

What Sets the Dolomites Apart?

Many mountains are impressive. These fascinate. They tell stories, provide culinary treats mid-hike, and offer you a glass of Hugo or Schiava wine when you least expect it. Here, the barrier between nature and culture is completely blurred.

- Effort meets elegance: One trail climbs to a panoramic cross over Alta Badia, and the descent concludes at a rifugio serving fresh apple strudel. You hike through heat and dust before sitting down to a flawlessly prepared polenta with porcini.

- Accessible adventure: You don't have to be a climber to experience the wilderness here. Cable cars facilitate access to high terrain, allowing even families to experience what it's like to wander above the clouds.
- Multi-day magic: There's nowhere better for hut-to-hut trekking. Sleep on a high. Wake up to the dawn touching pink limestone. Eat pasta on a patio with views that feel surreal.

An Invitation, not a Checklist

The Dolomites just ask for attention. They do not require summits or quick paces. Whether it's a two-hour meadow loop or a nine-day trek along the Alta Via 1, the trail welcomes everyone. There are no "conquered" peaks here; only places to travel through, remember, and return to.

And that is the secret magic: there is never just one trip. The Dolomites leave strands behind, threads that will tug again the next season, year, or perhaps soon. These mountains continue to call even after you have been through them.

Get Oriented

Location and Geography

Understanding the Dolomites entails discovering how many universes may exist inside a single mountain range. This is not a single park or territory, but rather a tangled stretch of peaks and valleys sculpted by glaciers, war, herders, and language differences. The Dolomites are not so much a destination but a multifaceted world woven together by history and stone.

They connect three provinces—South Tyrol (Alto Adige), Trentino, and Belluno—and two autonomous regions: Trentino-Alto Adige/Südtirol and Veneto. That intricacy is important. Not just on a map, but right under your feet. Trails may begin in a Ladin-speaking hamlet, wind through German-speaking fields, and conclude in an Italian rifugio serving pasta al pomodoro. It's part of what makes trekking here feel like a journey across time as well as terrain.

- **Where exactly are the Dolomites?**

Geographically, the Dolomites are located in northeastern Italy, on the natural border between the Germanic Alps and the Italian Apennines. They extend approximately from the Adige River in the west (between Bolzano and Trento) to the Piave River in the east (beyond Belluno). They run from the Austrian border to the Venetian plains.

The core area nominated by UNESCO as a World Heritage Site comprises approximately 142,000 hectares and is divided into nine separate mountain ranges, including:

- Pelmo and Croda da Lago
- Marmolada (the Dolomites' highest peak at 3,343 meters)
- Puez-Odle
- Catinaccio/Latemar

- Tre Cime di Lavaredo
- Pale di San Martino
- Fanes-Sennes-Braies
- Schlern-Rosengarten
- Brenta Dolomites

Each system has its own personality—some wild and jagged, some soft-shouldered and pastoral, and some with a difficult history to ignore.

Knowing the lay of the terrain is not only beneficial to hikers, but also necessary. This is a region where cable cars, rifugi, language, signage, and even cuisine change with each pass and valley. Orientation is more than just geographical; it is also cultural and utilitarian.

The Parks

The Dolomites are surrounded by various national and regional parks, each of which protects a portion of its natural and historical wealth. Some are huge and provide multi-day wilderness adventures. Others are more personal, concentrating on geology, flora, or specific cultural areas.

- **Natural Park Fanes-Sennes-Braies (South Tyrol)**

This park is one of the largest and most popular in the region, and it is ideal for hut-to-hut trekking. It includes high plateaus, karst landscapes, and alpine lakes such as Lago di Braies, whose emerald mirror has become a symbol in its own right. Rifugi like Fodara Vedla and Sennes are nestled deep inside its folds, providing access to secluded routes and wildlife encounters.

- **Natural Park Puez-Odle (South Tyrol)**

This is geology at full show. The Odle Group, with its sawtooth spires, rises abruptly over Val di Funes and Val Gardena. The Puez Plateau above Colfosco is a moonscape of quiet and fossils, and one of the best day walks in the Dolomites. Access is via cable car or steep climbs from Santa Cristina, Selva, or La Villa.

- **Natural Park Sciliar-Catinaccio (South Tyrol)**

Legends and light thrive here. The Sciliar massif, with its flat summit and vertical walls, towers over Alpe di Siusi. The Catinaccio/Rosengarten mountain glows orange at sunset; the name "rose garden" comes from a local legend. Trails here wind through forests, meadows, and breathtaking ridge treks that equal anything in the Alps.

- **Parco Paneveggio, Pale di San Martino (Trentino)**

Wilder, less frequented, and more moody. The Pale Plateau above San Martino di Castrozza is a barren, treeless landscape of rock and quiet. Down below, the Paneveggio Forest produces violins from spruce wood originally used by Stradivari. Trails here feel ancient, remote, and completely unscripted.

- **Dolomiti Bellunesi National Park, Veneto**

This park, located on the southeastern edge of the Dolomites, veers into an untamed area. There are few tourists. There are few cable cars. The steep valleys and deep gorges make it ideal for the more self-sufficient hiker. Trailheads are dispersed, but the payoff is solitude and nature at its most raw.

Valleys and Mountain Hubs

The Dolomites are not a single range, but rather a collection of peaks separated by valleys, which create the trekking experience. Where you establish yourself influences the type of trails, logistics, culture, and even language you'll encounter.

- **Val Gardena, South Tyrol**

A hiker's fortress. This valley, which includes Ortisei, Santa Cristina, and Selva di Val Gardena, connects directly to the Seceda ridgelines, the Sassolungo Group, and the Puez-Odle gateway. Lifts and public transportation are easily accessible, and there is a strong Ladin cultural presence. There are plenty of shops, outdoor stores, and rifugi access.

- **Alta Badia (South Tyrol)**

More refined and less boisterous. Trailheads to the core of the Dolomites, particularly Sella, Puez, and Fanes, may be found in towns such as La Villa, Corvara, and Colfosco. The rifugi here frequently lean gourmet, and the trails combine high alpine drama with Ladin charm.

- **Val di Fassa, Trentino**

A picturesque valley flanked by the Catinaccio, Marmolada, and Sella peaks. Hikers, climbers, and mountain bikers flock to towns like Canazei, Pozza di Fassa, and Campitello during the summer months. From here, you may get to Passo Pordoi, Passo Sella, and several more important Alta Via links.

- **Cortina d'Ampezzo, Veneto**

Cortina is not only stylish, but also trail-rich. Hike from here to Cinque Torri, Tofane, Cristallo, and the western flanks of Tre Cime. A useful base for both day treks and Via Ferrata. Infrastructure is decent, however, more car-dependent than other of the South Tyrolean cities.

- **San Martino di Castrozza, Trentino.**

This little village, nestled beneath the Pale of San Martino, is vastly underrated. Excellent access to hut-to-hut trails through the Pale Plateau and Paneveggio Park. Fewer crowds, more wilderness.

- **Dobbiaco and Sesto (South Tyrol)**

Ideal for those looking for Tre Cime di Lavaredo, Lago di Landro, and the high plateaus around Rifugio Locatelli. These upper Puster Valley settlements are quieter than Cortina and provide easier access to the northern peaks.

- **Alleghe and Civetta, Belluno**

Alleghe, located on the slopes of Monte Civetta, offers lakefront serenity surrounded by high cliffs. Civetta's sheer walls dominate, and there is excellent access to distant paths and climbs, but with less developed tourist infrastructure.

Language

Language in the Dolomites is more than simply signage; it's the soul.

This region is one of Europe's most linguistically diverse. There are three primary languages spoken in different combinations depending on the valley and province:

- German is predominantly spoken in South Tyrol (Alto Adige), particularly in Val Gardena, Val Pusteria, and many northern districts. Expect to encounter German as the primary language on signs, menus, and trail markers.

- Italian is the dominant language of Trentino and Belluno, and it is spoken across the Dolomites, particularly in Cortina, Val di Fassa, and San Martino.
- Ladin, an ancient Rhaeto-Romance language, is spoken in areas such as Val Badia, Val Gardena, and Val di Fassa. It serves as a bridge between Latin and Alpine languages, shaping the region's cultural legacy.

Trail signs are sometimes trilingual, including German, Italian, and Ladin (e.g., Grödner Tal / Val Gardena / Gherdëina). Rifugio employees typically speak at least two languages, and sometimes three. English is frequently spoken in tourist regions, but trail markers and maps nearly always use local names; understanding them is important.

This entails being aware of two (or three) names:

- Ortisei/St. Ulrich/Urtijëi
- Sella Pass | Passo Sella / Jëuf de Sela.
- Tre Cime di Lavaredo / Drei Zinnen

Orientation Tips That Matter

- Maps: Always pack a physical map (tabacco maps are the gold standard). Digital programs such as Komoot or Outdooractive can be useful, although phone signals often fade in valleys or behind rock faces.
- Transport logic: Do not underestimate the distances between hubs. A trail from Cortina may appear near Val Gardena on the map, but driving there could take three hours.
- Elevation realities: Cable cars transform everything. Knowing where lifts are, when they operate, and which trails connect above 2,000 meters is critical to better route planning.
- Booking wisely: Rifugi in great demand (such as Locatelli, Lagazuoi, and Nuvolau) require early reservations. Know which huts are CAI or AVS, and what membership savings are available.

When to Visit

The timing of a hike in the Dolomites is not determined by availability; rather, it is determined by the type of world you want to enter.

The collection expresses its seasons loudly. Snowmelt reveals high alpine meadows as June arrives, while October turns the larch woods gold. In between is a dance of warmth, thunder, blooms, lengthy twilight walks, and ephemeral tranquillity. The trail itself may stay the same, but its soul changes every few weeks.

- **June**

The trails start to breathe again. Snow clings on high passes, but lower valleys and mid-altitude roads are blooming with wildflowers. Edelweiss, alpine asters, and fireweed adorn the meadows. Rifugi will eventually open. Early in the month, several higher cable cars were still awaiting clearance, but by mid-June, most access points were operational.

Ideal for: Flower seekers, quieter trekking, and lower-altitude circuits such as Alpe di Siusi, Val Fiscalina, and Val di Funes.

- **July**

Peak bloom and peak beauty. Meltwater causes river levels to rise. The entire spectrum seems energized. Rifugi are operating at full capacity, and all important routes, including Alta Vias, are accessible. The weather can change quickly:

hot one day, afternoon storms the next. Nonetheless, skies regularly clear, resulting in artistic evenings.

Ideal for: Long trail days, full-access Alta Vias, rifugi stays, alpine lake treks, and photography.

- **August**

The summer is lush and full. Also, the busiest. Italians, Germans, Austrians, and others pack the valleys for ferragosto and mountain vacations. Trails around hubs such as Tre Cime or Seceda turn into foot traffic highways by late morning. The upside? Culture is alive. Ladin festivals take place. Music echoes across valley chapels. Mountain food is at its pinnacle.

Best for: Comprehensive Dolomite trekking, hut-to-hut excursions, and cultural immersion.

- **September**

The silence returns. Temperatures drop, but the larches begin to change. The valleys are filled with tranquility. With schools back in session and summer crowds thinned down, this is the ideal hour for those seeking privacy. Rifugis are open until mid- to late September, depending on snow forecasts.

Best for: Alta Via finishers, autumn color hikes, and anyone who enjoys soft light and serenity.

- **October (early only)**

The door is closing. Some huts are still open for weekend warriors and daytrippers. Lower elevation trails are still dry. By mid-October, snowfall is a genuine probability at elevations above 2,000 meters. However, early October hikes—particularly in Val di Funes, Rosengarten, and around Lago di Braies—are among the most photogenic of the year.

Ideal for: autumn color treks, day hikes around towns, and low-valley pastoral paths.

Snowline, Trail Closure, and Elevation Logic

The Dolomites' elevation is easily underestimated. The distances between valleys may be minor, but trails frequently rise sharply into snow zones that stay blocked well into June.

- Above 2,500 meters, expect snow until early July. Crampons are not usually required, although vigilance is essential.
- Between 2,000 and 2,500 meters: These are the ideal trekking locations—mostly clean by mid-June and dry into September.

- Below 2,000 meters: Ideal for shoulder season hiking (late spring to early fall), particularly near San Candido, Alleghe, and Val di Fassa.

Rifugi often provides trail updates, and the CAI (Club Alpino Italiano) website lists closures. Many Alta Via parts are not suggested until the middle of July. Always check locally.

Festival Tie-Ins: Where culture meets the trail

The Dolomites not only provide entertainment with their splendor, but also nourish the spirit with their traditions. Festivals emerge like wildflowers throughout the summer:

- Sagra di San Giacomo (Val Badia): A Ladin feast featuring traditional attire, outdoor music, and home-cooked mountain cuisine.
- Transumanza (South Tyrol and Trentino): The ritual herding of cattle down from summer pastures, frequently accompanied by parades, yodels, and butter-slathered bread.
- Almabtrieb (Val di Funes, September): Decorated cows, mountain music, and plum cake signal the end of the grazing season.

- Rifugi Concert Series (Alta Badia): Open-air classical and jazz concerts held in mountain huts—why not have cello with your strudel?

Walking through these traditions transforms a hiking trip into a living anthropology course—but not the type that ends with beer and dumplings.

Types of Hiking Experiences

Day Hikes versus Multi-Day Treks

The Dolomites cater to both campfire dreamers and casual wanderers. Some visitors never spend a night above 2,000 meters, yet return astounded. Others spend a week tracing ridge lines, never touching the pavement. There is no wrong approach.

- Day Hikes

Ideal for those living in a single valley or town. Hikers can get to alpine basins and ridge trails in minutes thanks to dozens of cable car lines.

- Seceda Ridgeline (Val Gardena): Postcard view. Short loop or full-day variation.
- Lago di Sorapis (Cortina): A blue-glass lake in a limestone basin.
- Puez-Odle Traverse: High-altitude vista connecting Colfosco and Selva via Rifugio Puez.

Ideal for: Families, first-timers, photographers, and time-conscious travelers.

- Multi-Day Treks

This is where the true spirit of Dolomite hiking manifests itself.

- Alta Via 1 is the most accessible of the long-distance routes. Begins at Lago di Braies and concludes in Belluno. 8-10 days.

- Alta Via 2: More distant, tricky, and tough. For experienced trekkers.
- Alta Via 3-6: Lesser known and wilder. Less infrastructure. Some require bivouac experience.

Each Alta Via connects high passes, rifugi, and storybook scenery. Expect to spend 6-10 hours on the path each day, with communal camping and family-style meals served above the clouds.

Themed Hiking Routes

- WWI History Trails

The Dolomites were a harsh front in World War I. To survive, soldiers blasted passages through rock, tunneled under peaks, and created via ferrata.

- Lagazuoi Tunnels: Descend through the very rock that warriors fought on.
- Cinque Torri ditches: Explore restored ditches alongside towering stone towers.
- Monte Piana is a large battleground turned summit. Somber and stirring.
- Panoramic Ridge Hikes

The kind of terrain where a break every ten steps feels necessary.

- Seceda to Rifugio Florence.
- Col dei Bos Ridge (Above Cortina)
- Sasso Piatto Circuit (Val Gardena)

Views span half the range. For layered light, shoot early or late in the day.

- Family-friendly Trails

These are not the flat walkways of a municipal park. These are pathways that both children and grandparents will enjoy—shorter distances, easy grades, and alpine chalets and cows at the end.

- Alpe di Siusi loops
- Val Fiscalina - Rifugio Fondovalle
- Col Raiser to Rifugio Juac (with a playground stop)

Most begin at lift stations, reducing elevation gain while increasing scenery.

- Alpine Lake Loops

Water this blue should not be real. But here it is, surrounded by peaks and reflected perfectly.

- Lago di Braies: An easy loop, best done early in the morning.
- Lago di Sorapis: Moderate difficulty, turquoise payoff.
- Lago di Limedes: Small, magical, and rarely crowded.

Ideal for hikers looking for peaceful sparkling waters at sunrise or dusk.

At the Edge of the Map

This isn't the type of range where one home base suffices. The Dolomites encourage movement through valleys, over passes, and from village to hamlet. They reward hiking that reads like a tale, with several chapters, changing characters, and a landscape that reinvents itself with each turn.

Being orientated here means paying attention rather than remembering names. Accents in a shop. Menu at a rifugio. The trail signs change from German to Italian with altitude. The way light falls in Val di Funes differs from Val di Fassa. The Dolomites communicate in a variety of languages, but they all tell the same thing: keep traveling and look intently.

Planning Your Trip

Hiking in the Dolomites isn't about checking off places. It's about developing a rhythm. A slow, forceful cadence that travels with the mountain light, lunches at a rifugio table, and the rising mist from a trailhead. The challenge is not where to go, but how to choose, connect, and go deep without rushing.

Whether you're there for three days or ten, the Dolomites reward careful planning. What follows is not a rigorous blueprint, but rather a collection of tried-and-true pathways that are full of possibilities. This is the planning foundation that brings the trails to life when combined with smart base choices, hotel options for every type of hiker, and practical booking suggestions.

Recommended Hiking Routes

3 Days: Taste and Tease

For those with limited time, the goal is immersion, not mileage. Concentrate on a single massif. Allow the trails to unveil themselves gently.

Option A: Seceda and the Odle Group (Val Gardena Base)

- Day 1: Cable car to Seceda, ridge walk to Rifugio Firenze and back.
- Day 2: Odle Panorama Trail from Col Raiser to Brogles Alm; loop along woodland pathways.
- Day 3: Alpe di Siusi meadow walk; lunch at Gostner Schwaige.

Ideal for: First-time Dolomite hikers, photographers, and families seeking gentle terrain with spectacular views.

Option B: Lagazuoi and Cinque Torri (Cortina Base).

- Day 1: WWI Museum Loop at Cinque Torri.
- Day 2: Lagazuoi cable car, tunnel descent, overnight stay at Rifugio Lagazuoi.
- Day 3: Passo Falzarego Ridge Trail or Forcella Averau trek.

Ideal for: History buffs and hikers seeking drama without committing to big distances.

5 days: Ridge to Refuge

Five days allow for hut-to-hut exploration without complete Alta Via commitment. You can either base yourself in two locations or anchor deeply in one and travel outside.

Recommended Flow: Civetta + Pelmo

- Day 1: Arrive in Alleghe; brief warm-up climb to Lago Coldai.
- Day 2: Trek to Rifugio Tissi via Coldai saddle, and overnight beneath Civetta's wall.
- Day 3: descent via Val Civetta and transfer to Passo Staulanza.
- Day 4: The Monte Pelmo loop (via Rifugio Venezia and Forcella d'Arcia)
- Day 5: Short hike to dinosaur traces, or rest day in Val di Zoldo.

Ideal for hikers seeking seclusion, alpine scale, and less-traveled paths.

7 Day: The Great Traverse Lite

One week enables serious exploration. Combine traditional routes with quieter terrain. Combine plateaus, cliffs, and lakes.

Suggested Flow: Alta Badia, Fanes, Seceda

- Day 1: Base at La Villa, warm-up hike to Santa Croce Sanctuary.
- Day 2: Capanna Alpina to Fanes Plateau; stay overnight at Rifugio Fanes.
- Day 3: Ju de Limo loop to Lavarella, return or overnight.
- Day 4: Transfer to Ortisei; ride Seceda lift, then trek ridge to Rifugio Firenze.
- Day 5: Rifugio to Brogles Alm traverse, then descend to Ortisei.
- Day 6: Alpe di Siusi full loop; stay in Malga Sanon.
- Day 7: Rosengarten day tour from Vigo di Fassa, or rest day.

Ideal for: Scenic enthusiasts, photographers, and first-time hut hikers.

10 Days of Full Immersion

A ten-day trip encompasses the entire spectrum—iconic and obscure, harsh and soft, mountain and meadow.

Recommended Flow: Alta Via 1 Southbound + Cortina Finale

- Day 1: Lake of Braies to Rifugio Biella.
- Day 2: Cross to Rifugio Fanes.
- Day 3: Continue to Rifugio Lagazuoi.
- Day 4: descent to Passo Falzarego and transfer to Cinque Torri.
- Day 5: Cinque Torri - Rifugio Nuvolau and Averau
- Day 6: Visit the Croda da Lago circuit; stay overnight at Rifugio Palmieri.
- Day 7: descend to Cortina; overnight in town.
- Day 8: Hike to Tofana di Rozes from Rifugio Dibona.
- Day 9: Rosengarten Circuit (by Shuttle to Vigo)
- Day 10: Return to Venice or Bolzano.

Ideal for: Strong hikers, bucket listers, and Alta Via dreamers who do not intend to complete the entire trek.

Best Home Bases by Interest

Every Dolomite base has its own personality. Choose your anchor based not only on accessibility, but also on the type of days and evenings you prefer.

Cortina D'Ampezzo

- Best for: Drama, high-alpine views, WWI history, access to Tofane, Cinque Torri, and Lagazuoi.

- Pros: Iconic vistas, excellent dining scene, via ferrata alternatives.
- Watch out for: High costs during high season; reserving early is necessary.

Ortisei (Val Gardena)

- Best for Seceda, Alpe di Siusi, family-friendly treks, and culture.
- Pros: Ladin charm, decent transportation links, lift access directly from town.
- Bonus: Art galleries, woodcarving tradition, and delicious pastries.

Selva di Val Gardena

- Ideal for: Alta Via 2 access, Sella Group, Puez-Odle Park.
- Pros: More alpine than Ortisei; stronger for technical hikers.
- Works well as a starting or finishing point for hut-to-hut tours.

San Candido (Innichen)

- Best for: Tre Cime, Dolomiti di Sesto, and Lake Braies.

- Pros: Quieter than Cortina; direct train connections to Austria.
- Ideal for: Hikers who desire alpine without overexposure.

Alleghe

- Ideal for: Monte Civetta, Coldai, Tissi, and lesser-known AV1 parts.
- Pros: Lakefront charm and uncrowded paths.
- Note: A car simplifies logistics here.

San Martino di Castrozza

- Ideal for: Pale di San Martino, Rosetta Plateau.
- Pros: A gateway to one of the Dolomites' wilder places.
- Base for high stillness, an unspoiled landscape, and fewer crowds.

How to Combine Regions without Excessive Travel

Here's when solid planning pays off. The Dolomites aren't particularly large, but distances may be misleading—twisting mountain roads, lift connections, and transportation changes all add up.

Here's how you can move efficiently between zones:

- Lifts or short drives connect Seceda, Alpe di Siusi, and Rosengarten, with bases in Ortisei or Selva.
- From Fanes to Cortina and Cinque Torri, a single base in Cortina allows for strategic day visits to all destinations.
- Alta Via 1 partials ↔ Braies ↔ Civetta: Begin at Braies, climb south, and finish at Alleghe
- From Pale di San Martino to Val di Fassa and Rosengarten, stay overnight in Vigo di Fassa for shuttle access.
- Use hubs like Bolzano, Brunico, and Dobbiaco as bridges between areas, especially when combining train and bus travel.

Transfer Tips:

- Aim for two primary bases during a seven or ten-day trip.
- Limit region-hopping to every 3-4 days to maximize trail time.

- Luggage services are scarce; pack light if going frequently.
- Rental automobiles provide flexibility, although regional buses are good in summer.

Lodging Options in the Dolomites

The magic of hiking here isn't limited to the paths. It's where you sleep afterward—on high plateaus, in flowery fields, next to larch woods.

Mountain Rifugi (Huts)

- The most immersive choice—dorms or private rooms, big meals, shared tables
- Book at least three months in advance for July/August stays.
- Prices range from €50-80 for half-board (dorm) and €80-120 for private rooms.
- Open: Mid/late June - late September, sometimes until mid-October depending on snow.
- Booking sites include direct websites, regional portals, or phone/email.
- Not to miss: Rifugio Fanes, Tissi, Florence, Lagazuoi, and Pradidali.

Agriturismi and Bed and Breakfasts

- Locally owned farm stays or small inns, especially in valley communities.
- Ideal for post-hut nights, picturesque bases, or hike-light days.
- Serve local cuisine—polenta, speck, and homemade jams.
- Prices range from around €60-120 per room/night.
- Found in: Val Badia, Val di Fassa, and Val di Zoldo.

Alpine Hotels and Guesthouses

- Higher comfort, frequently with spa/wellness amenities.
- Located in bigger towns (Cortina, Ortisei, San Candido).
- Ideal for combining hiking with leisure.
- Book early for Cortina, Ortisei, and San Cassiano.

Campsites and Vanlife

- Excellent in the Alta Pusteria, Val di Funes, and Alleghe areas.
- Clean, well-managed, sometimes with cafes and hot showers.

- Wild camping is forbidden in the majority of the Dolomites.

How to Book Rifugi (and When Do They Open)

Rifugio planning is an art. Done correctly, it unlocks the most satisfying version of the Dolomites—where you may watch the sunset from a ridge, sleep behind stone walls, and wake up to silence and alpenglow.

When Do Rifugis Open?

- Main Season: Mid-June to Late September.
- Some remain open until early October if weather permits.
- High snow years can delay openings until early July.

How to Book

- Book directly: Most rifugi accept reservations via website or email.
- Some accept internet platforms, such as rifugi.cai.it and Booking for private huts.
- Request in Ladin, German, or Italian for faster responses (Google Translate helps).
- Confirm the arrival time, bed type (dorm/private), meals, payment (many are cash-only).

- Follow-up: Some huts confirm manually; don't hesitate to email again after 48 hours.

What to Bring

- Sleeping sheet or liner (required in dorms).
- Most high huts only accept cash, not credit cards.
- Earplugs, torch, and a small towel
- Light pack—rifugi provides blankets, food, and water.

Cancellation

- Most have flexible regulations about the weather.
- No-shows without notification? Frequently charged or barred from future stays.

Book early for

- Rifugio Lagazuoi, Tissi, Re Alberto, and Lavarella: July-August books quickly.
- Alta Via trekkers: Plan cottages before flights, as availability influences your path.

Final Thought: Designing a Journey, Not Just a Trip

The Dolomites do not need to be conquered. They're not about collecting summits or ticking off peaks. They are about meaningful movement—trails that alter not only one's perspective but also one's emotional state.

So, plan your vacation such that you don't have to hustle and instead listen to the pace of the landscape. Allow space on your plan for misty mornings, dinners that take longer than intended, and detours into forest clearings or mountain stillness.

Getting There and Around

Regardless of how isolated or steep their summits appear, the Dolomites are surprisingly approachable. Reaching this region of the Alps, however, is more than just transportation; it's about understanding the flow, knowing how to connect quickly, and feeling at ease on roads that twist dramatically beneath rock walls and through alpine valleys. With the correct logistics, travel may be transformed from a frustrating necessity to a vital and joyful element of your Dolomite experience.

Here's how to navigate with ease, confidence, and delight.

Closest Airports

Choosing the right airport to start your excursion sets the tone for the entire journey. Each gateway provides various benefits based on your trip plans, itinerary, and preferred first stops.

Venice Marco Polo Airport (VCE)

- Ideal for: The quickest direct route to Cortina, Alta Badia, and the eastern Dolomites.
- Cortina is about a 2-hour drive or bus ride away.

Pros:

- There are frequent international flights with good connections from North America and Europe.
- Drive scenically and quickly to Belluno via the A27 freeway.
- Reliable public transportation connections (Cortina Express, ATVO).

Tip: Make small stops en route in lovely places such as Conegliano for coffee or snacks.

Innsbruck Airport (INN)

- Ideal for the northern Dolomites, including Val Gardena, Alta Pusteria, Tre Cime, and Ortisei.
- Driving to Val Gardena or Dobbiaco takes 1.5 hours.

Pros:

- A small, easy-to-navigate airport with Alpine flair.
- Shorter routes to northern valleys and less traffic.
- Regular rail services run from Innsbruck Hauptbahnhof to Bolzano, Bressanone, and Brunico.

Tip: Innsbruck is an enjoyable overnight stay, with attractive streets, Tyrolean culture, and mountain vistas just outside the station.

Verona Airport (VRN)

- Ideal for the southern and western Dolomites, including Trentino, Val di Fassa, and Pale di San Martino.
- Travel time by automobile to Val di Fassa or San Martino di Castrozza is approximately 2.5 hours.

Pros:

- Less congested than Venice and easily accessible via the A22 road.
- There are good international flight options from the United Kingdom and Europe, as well as regional flights within Italy.

Tip: Verona's old town, located just a short distance from the airport, provides superb culture and gastronomy for those looking for a leisurely introduction.

Munich Airport (MUC)

- Ideal for those looking for a leisurely road trip through the Bavarian Alps on their way to the Dolomites.
- Travel time by automobile is 3-4 hours, depending on the location.

Pros:

- A wide range of foreign flight options are available at cheap prices.
- Beautiful journey via Bavaria, Innsbruck, and the Brenner Pass.
- There are frequent train connections between Innsbruck and Bolzano.

Tip: Munich is best suited for those planning longer trips or those looking to combine Dolomite trekking with other mountain adventures.

Train Connections and Mountain Transfers

Because of its rugged geography, the Dolomites region does not have substantial direct rail service, but trains are still an excellent option for getting to the region before shifting to more localized transit.

Primary Rail Entry Points:

- Bolzano/Bozen is convenient for Val Gardena, Ortisei, and the western Dolomites.
- Brunico/Bruneck serves as the gateway to Alta Pusteria, San Candido, and the Tre Cime di Lavaredo.
- Belluno or Calalzo di Cadore: Ideal for Cortina d'Ampezzo and the eastern Dolomites.
- Bressanone/Brixen is ideal for direct bus connections to Val di Funes and Val Gardena.

Transfer from Train to Trail:

- Regular public buses (SAD and Dolomitibus) connect these stations with smaller towns and trailheads.

- Private taxi services and scheduled mountain transfers are readily available, making them ideal for large groups or those carrying big luggage.

Smart Tip

- Trains should arrive around lunchtime for a smoother journey. Buses are more regular, and daylight makes finding lodging easy and scenic.

Car Rental Tips: Freedom and Responsibility

Having a rental car in the Dolomites provides unparalleled freedom—discover hidden valleys, secluded trailheads, and lovely communities at your leisure. However, driving in the Dolomites necessitates caution, patience, and adherence to local norms.

Understanding ZTL zones (Zona Traffico Limitato)

- Many historic towns (such as Bolzano and Cortina) have ZTLs—restricted driving zones enforced by automatic cameras.
- Entering these regions without a permit might result in heavy fines.
- Watch out for ZTL indicators. If you are hesitant, park outside the town center and walk or take a shuttle in.

Mountain Driving: Safe and enjoyable.

- The roads across mountain passes (Passo Gardena, Falzarego, Sella) are twisting, beautiful, and small. Speed limits (typically 50-70 km/h) indicate the need for prudence.
- Summer traffic on popular roads can be considerable; early morning or late-day travel reduces congestion.
- Weather in high passes varies rapidly. Carry layers, snacks, and a map in case of an unexpected delay.

Tip: Take your time, pull over to appreciate the scenery, and let quicker locals pass.

Parking Considerations

- High season parking (July-August) at trailheads (Lago di Braies, Tre Cime, Seceda) fills up quickly by 8-9 AM.
- Many lots require payment (usually in coins only).

Tip: Before going to the trailhead, look for parking options online. Arrive early or take shuttles from the valley towns.

Cable Cars and Funivia

Cable cars (funivia) are more than just a convenience; they are integral to the Dolomite hiking culture, allowing hikers of all fitness levels to visit stunning high-altitude paths and panoramic summits.

Recommended Cable Cars by Region

- Cortina attractions include Tofana di Mezzo (Freccia nel Cielo), the Faloria cableway, and the Cinque Torri lift.
- Val Gardena: Seceda funivia, Col Raiser gondola, and Sassolungo's distinctive standing gondola (Passo Sella).
- Alta Badia: Piz La Ila and the Boè lift for the Sellaronda paths.
- San Martino di Castrozza: The Rosetta cableway leads to the Pale di San Martino plateau.

Seasonal operation

- Most lifts are open from mid-June to late September/early October, weather permitting.
- A handful reopen in the winter (mainly ski-oriented).
- Always double-check specific dates and times online or at local tourism offices before arriving.

Cable Car Tips

- Early morning lifts beat the throng and provide calm trails.
- If you plan on spending many days in the mountains, consider purchasing multi-day lift cards or Dolomiti Supersummer passes.
- During peak season (July/August), purchasing tickets online ahead of time allows you to avoid waits at popular lifts such as Seceda or Tre Cime.

Public Transport vs. Rental Car

While rental automobiles provide complete flexibility, public transportation in the Dolomites is extremely efficient, environmentally friendly, and surprisingly extensive. Making the appropriate pick is determined by your itinerary style.

Regional Bus Networks and Passes

- SAD, Dolomitibus, and Cortina Express: These buses connect all the valleys and popular trails.
- Timetables are well-maintained online (for example, altoadigemobilita.info), and tourist offices freely provide easy-to-follow printed schedules.

- The DolomitiMobil Card provides unlimited travel on regional buses and some trains, making it especially useful for those who utilize public transportation on a daily basis. Purchase via tourism offices, stations, or online.

Advantages of Public Transportation

- Economical, eco-friendly, and stress-free.
- During peak summer, buses frequently enter areas that are off-limits to private cars (Lago di Braies, Tre Cime).
- Integrated with regional train networks to provide easy transfers.

When Renting a Car Makes Sense

- Staying in rural agriturismi or remote cottages with minimal bus service.
- Flexible itinerary requiring unplanned detours or less-visited trailheads.
- Comfortable with mountain driving and logistics.

Best practices for combined travel

- Use public transportation to travel between towns and to access popular trails.

- Rent a car just for rural portions or to drive between geographically distant areas (such as Cortina and San Martino di Castrozza).

Dolomiti Mobility Cards: Comfort in Your Pocket

These regional cards are more than just paper passes; they improve your travel experience, allow for spontaneous route modifications, and encourage slower, deeper travel through the valleys. Here are the best options to consider:

Mobilcard Südtirol

- Coverage includes all regional trains and buses in South Tyrol (Val Gardena, Val di Funes, Alta Pusteria, Bolzano, and Bressanone).
- Duration options include 1, 3, and 7 days.
- Where to get it: Tourist information centers, online, or included in some hotel stays.
- Why it's useful: Ideal for people who don't have a car and want to stay in Ortisei, Selva, or San Candido.

Guest Pass: Val Gardena, Val di Fassa, and Alta Badia.

- What it is: Some hotels and guesthouses include local mobility cards in the room charge; check before booking.

- Access: Local buses, ski lifts in the summer (depending on location), and certain museum admissions.
- Best for: Basecamp travelers planning day treks from a single town.

Dolomiti Super Summer Card

- Ideal for hikers planning many lift trips.
- Coverage: 120+ lifts in 12 Dolomite valleys.
- Pass types include day passes and points cards.
- Flexibility: Use throughout various valleys, ideal for treks or extended stays.

Cortina Pass/Summer Card

- Specific to Cortina d'Ampezzo and its surroundings.
- Inclusions include public transit discounts, elevator access packages, and museum admission.
- Combine with: Regional buses on the Lagazuoi, Tre Cime, and WWI lines.

Tips for Moving Smoothly over the Mountains

The Dolomites reward those who plan, but also those who plan lightly enough to allow for flexibility. Here's how to travel efficiently between towns, valleys, and trailheads without wasting time or energy.

Plan shifts between towns wisely

- Mornings are ideal, especially when changing bases. Afternoon buses are generally infrequent, and trail beginnings wane until dinnertime.
- Base shift days are rest days; use transfer days for short trekking or rifugio-to-town transition trips. Unless you're exceptionally fit and experienced, avoid racking up a lot of miles on move days.
- Avoid significant transfers on Sundays due to limited service across areas. Always double-check Sunday/holiday transit schedules.

Understand Road Rhythms

- Market days in communities like San Candido and Ortisei might result in road closures or traffic delays.
- Late July and August bring holiday crowds and limited parking at key trailheads; arrive by 7:30 a.m. or take public shuttles.
- Evenings in smaller towns frequently become quiet early. Plan to eat, refuel, and restock by late afternoon.

Use Trailheads as Natural Hubs

Many trailheads serve as natural transition sites, providing shuttle services, rifugi overnight stays, and access to the next valley. Build your itinerary to pass through these, and you'll be able to connect numerous places without ever going back.

Key Hubs to Consider:

- Passo Gardena: Links Alta Badia → Val Gardena
- Passo Falzarego: Cortina to Alta Badia/Lagazuoi zone.
- Capanna Alpina: The gateway to Fanes from San Cassiano.
- Passo Rolle: connects Pale di San Martino with the Trentino valley.
- Tre Cime parking lot (Auronzo): Northern AV1 start, entrance to Lake Misurina.

Information on Taxis and Private Transfers

While expensive, private transports across valleys can bridge difficult logistical gaps, particularly for groups. Most can be pre-booked through your hotel or area shuttle services.

- South Tyrol has a modern taxi network (frequently included on regional tourism websites).
- Alta Pusteria and Cortina offer shared shuttle services for AV1 drop-offs and hut returns.

Smart use: A private transport can save you 2-3 bus transfers, which is worth it if time is of the essence or the weather is changing.

In the end, travel becomes a trail.

In the Dolomites, the journey begins when you leave the airport, not at the trailhead. The trip includes the drive up into a valley, the slow turn around a cliff-side pass, and the first sight of a jagged horizon bursting through the clouds.

There's no reason to overengineer every detail. The Dolomites do not reward precise planning, but rather smart instincts, patient movement, and curiosity. Whether you arrive with train tickets or only a pack and an idea, the most important thing is that you arrive.

Top Hiking Destinations

Tre Cime di Lavaredo & Surroundings

There are mountain icons, and then there's the Tre Cime di Lavaredo. Three massive limestone sentinels rise like chiseled teeth into the alpine sky, creating what could be the most photographed skyline in the Dolomites. But what's the real secret? They are not only stunningly beautiful, but also incredibly accessible.

Whether walking the classic loop trail, exploring WWI tunnels and trenches, or connecting to the larger expanse of the Sesto Dolomites, this area provides a hiking experience rich in awe, history, and high-mountain atmosphere. The moment the peaks appear from Rifugio Auronzo, it is clear that this is more than just a trail. It is a pilgrimage.

Scan for a GPS-Enabled Map Experience

Trail overviews

1. Classic Tre Cime Loop (Ring Trail)

67

- Route: Rifugio Auronzo - Forcella Lavaredo - Rifugio Locatelli - Malga Langalm - Rifugio Auronzo.
- Loop distance: around 10 kilometers.
- Duration: 3-4 hours (including time for photos and rifugi pauses).
- Elevation gain: approximately 350 m.
- Trail markers: CAI 101, 105, and 102.

This is the definitive circuit, the one on every hiker's list. But what distinguishes it is how swiftly it immerses. Within minutes of leaving Auronzo, the peaks emerge and never let go. The trail curves behind the spires, providing different viewpoints at each bend.

From Forcella Lavaredo, the vista north is expansive: Monte Paterno, Croda dei Toni, and the ridgelines of the Sesto group—all part of the WWI theater. The final stretch to Rifugio Locatelli provides a famous frontal view of the Tre Cime. It's a spot to sit, breathe, and listen to the solitude of the mountains.

2. Monte Paterno & WWI Tunnels

- Route: Rifugio Locatelli, Forcella Toblin, Via Ferrata Innerkofler, Monte Paterno Summit.

- Distance: around 4.5 kilometers round trip.
- Duration: three hours.
- Elevation gain: approximately 500 m.
- Technical requirements: Helmet, harness, and headlamp.

A voyage through the mountain's bones. Carved during World War I, the tunnel through Monte Paterno leads to a gloomy, dripping hallway of history. A headlamp is required because the path includes ladders and tight tunnels.

As we approached the top ridge, the Dolomites unfolded in full glory: the Cadini group, the distant Brenta Dolomites, and, of course, the menacing face of the Tre Cime—closer than ever. Not for the faint of heart, but a deep and thrilling journey through living history.

3. Lago di Landro to Tre Cime (for experienced hikers)

- Route: Val di Landro via Vallone di Rinbianco to Rifugio Auronzo.
- Distance: around 12 km one way.
- Duration: 5 hours uphill.
- Elevation gain: ~1000 meters.

For individuals who like to earn their views the hard way. The trail ascends from near Lago di Landro, passing through pine trees, scree fields, and scenic bends. Arriving in Auronzo this way enhances the first vista of the peaks. Highly suggested for a return loop that incorporates the traditional circuit.

Difficulty Levels

- Classic Loop: Moderate - appropriate for fit hikers, youngsters aged 8 and up, and confident beginners. The trail is wide in many places and well-marked, with some steep but manageable climbs.
- Monte Paterno / WWI Tunnels: Difficult / Technical - requires via ferrata experience, comfort with exposure, and suitable equipment. Not for casual hikers.
- Val di Landro ascent: Strenuous - long trek with steep sections; recommended for experienced hikers with a full day.

Highlights & Viewpoints

- Forcella Lavaredo: The first spectacular northward vista of the Tre Cime's vertical face, and arguably the most popular photo angle.
- Rifugio Locatelli terrace: Hikers halt for apple strudel and admire the wonderfully framed triple pillars.

- Monte Paterno peak offers a commanding 360° panorama that mixes military history and mountain prowess.
- Laghetti dei Piani: The little mountain lakes near Rifugio Locatelli that reflect the summits in still water—less visited but completely magnificent.
- Early morning light: The best views are between 7-9 a.m., when the peaks sparkle in low light and the throng have yet to arrive.

Access and Logistics

Trailhead: Rifugio Auronzo (2,333 metres)

How to reach it:

- To get there by car, take the toll road from Misurina, which is open from late June to early October for around €30 per vehicle.
- During the summer, shuttle buses run from Dobbiaco, Misurina, and Cortina d'Ampezzo.
- By foot: For experienced hikers, go Val di Landro or Val Fiscalina.

Parking: There are limited places at Auronzo, so arrive early (before 8 a.m.) in the busy season. The alternative is to park at Misurina and take the shuttle.

Best time to start: Early in the morning to avoid crowds and enjoy softer light. Late afternoon also rewards with sunset light, but time your return wisely.

Seasonal window: late June until early October. Early in the season, snow may persist on side routes.

Recommended Rifugi

Auronzo Mountain Refuge

- *At the trailhead*
- Indoor dining and terrace with Dolomite views.
- Starting point for the classic loop.
- Not for overnight unless arranged far in advance.

Refuge Lavaredo

- *A short walk from Auronzo*
- Excellent for a coffee break or lunch on the run.
- Cozier vibe; calmer in the early season.

Refugio Locatelli (Dreizinnenhütte)

- *Crown jewel of the road*
- Rustic but legendary, accommodations and dorms are booked months ahead.

- Serves local Ladin food in big servings.
- Open from June till late September.

Refuge Pian di Cengia

- *Tucked above Lake Piani*
- Less trafficked and good for overnight hikers.
- Connects easily with Monte Paterno and Innerkofler via ferrata.

Insider Tips

- Begin the circle counterclockwise, heading toward Rifugio Lavaredo. Most hikers move in this direction, and the views are more dramatic.
- Bring layers: Even in August, winds may be severe at Forcella Lavaredo and Locatelli. Storms develop swiftly in the afternoon.
- Stay overnight to see Tre Cime at sunset or morning without crowds. Rifugio Locatelli at sunrise is pure alchemy.
- Avoid midday in August; peak crowds arrive between 10:30am and 2:30pm. For peace and quiet, start your day at dawn or visit in September.

Few spots in the Dolomites produce such stunning results with so little initial work. Tre Cime is memorable not only for its splendor, but also for the way it incorporates tale, silence, and room to ponder. The trail rewards individuals who are unhurried, curious, and understand that hiking can occasionally include standing still.

Alta Via 1

Alta Via 1 is more than just a trail; it is a rite of passage. Known as the "classic" Dolomite high route, it encapsulates the essence of what makes these mountains famous: dramatic peaks, high-altitude meadows, historic rifugi, and ever-changing views.

This walk begins in the wonderfully gorgeous Lago di Braies and winds south for about 120 kilometers to the charming town of Belluno, passing through some of Europe's most breathtaking alpine vistas. It's a trek marked not only by footprints, but also by rhythm—day after day of early beginnings, afternoon thunderstorms, rifugi feasts, and evenings spent watching alpine glow soak into limestone cliffs.

Alta Via 1 exemplifies alpine hiking in its purest form: accessible, breathtaking, rewarding, and profoundly human.

Trail Overview and Route Details

- Starting Point: Lago di Braies (Pragser Wildsee), South Tyrol.
- Endpoint: Belluno (Veneto area)
- Length: about. 120 kilometers (~75 miles).
- Duration: Typically 8-11 days, depending on hiking speed and lodging availability.
- Total elevation gain: ~7,200 meters, including ascent and descent.
- Difficulty: Moderate to hard (suitable for fit hikers without technical climbing skills).
- The highest point is 2,752 meters at Forcella del Lago (near Rifugio Lagazuoi).
- Best hiking season: late June to mid-September.

Typical Stage Breakdown (example itinerary):

- Stage 1: Lago di Braies to Rifugio Biella/Sennes (3-5 hours).
- Stage 2: Rifugio Sennes to Rifugio Fanes (4-6 hours)
- Stage 3: Rifugio Fanes to Rifugio Lagazuoi (5-7 hours)
- Stage 4: Rifugio Lagazuoi to Rifugio Averau/Nuvolau (around 4-5 hours).
- Stage 5: Rifugio Averau/Nuvolau - Rifugio Città di Fiume (around 5-6 hours)

- Stage 6: Rifugio Città di Fiume - Rifugio Tissi (Civetta area, approximately 6-7 hours).
- Stage 7: Rifugio Tissi to Rifugio Carestiato (4-6 hours)
- Stage 8: Rifugio Carestiato to Rifugio Pian de Fontana (6-8 hours).
- Stage 9: Rifugio Pian de Fontana to Belluno (about 6-7 hours, descent to town).

Each day combines breathtaking scenery, comfy rifugi, and the pure thrill of alpine isolation. Paths are clearly designated with red and white CAI signs; route finding is simple, although maps or GPS apps improve the experience.

Difficulty Level and Trail Conditions

Scan for a GPS-Enabled Map Experience

Alta Via 1 is famous for being both accessible and rewarding. While technically non-demanding (no climbing gear or via ferrata equipment necessary), physical fitness and some prior multi-day hiking experience substantially boost enjoyment.

- Terrain: Mix of dirt tracks, rocky trails, scree slopes, sometimes steep ascents/descents.

- Exposure: Limited; some narrow paths, but no steep drops without a protective railing or cable support.
- Weather Sensitivity: Afternoon storms are typical; start early to prevent afternoon lightning strikes.

Highlights & Viewpoints

Alta Via 1 is continuously dazzling. Every stage has another iconic highlight:

- Lago di Braies: The emerald starting point is famously photogenic, especially in the early morning stillness.
- Fanes-Sennes-Braies Nature Park: Serene, rolling landscapes with brilliant wildflowers and wildlife sightings (marmots, ibex, golden eagles).
- Rifugio Lagazuoi has breathtaking views of the Tofane peaks and old WWI tunnels beneath the hut.
- Cinque Torri and Nuvolau are historic wartime trenches with panoramic views of the Dolomites.
- The north face of Monte Civetta is spectacularly vertical, often glowing rose-colored at sunset, and best viewed from Rifugio Tissi.
- Val di Zoldo and Belluno Dolomites: Less-traveled sections with silence and solitude, densely forested trails, and Veneto's cultural charm.

Recommended Rifugi (Mountain Huts)

Alta Via 1's allure is inextricably linked to its rifugio culture—comfortable alpine huts that serve hearty local meals, cozy beds, and companionship.

- Rifugio Biella (Day 1): Simple and isolated, the ideal first night stop.
- Rifugio Fanes (Day 2): Comfortable accommodations, gourmet cuisine, and a welcoming atmosphere.
- Rifugio Lagazuoi (Day 3): Stunning views, historical exhibitions, and a lively nighttime environment.
- Rifugio Averau/Nuvolau (Day 4): Two of the nicest shelters on the trail for food and scenery—the sunset here is amazing.
- Rifugio Città di Fiume (Day 5): A rustic charm beneath Monte Pelmo.
- Rifugio Tissi (Day 6): Unmatched Civetta face views, friendly hut keeper.
- Rifugio Carestiato (Day 7): Cozy setting, homemade pastries, and tranquil surroundings.
- Rifugio Pian de Fontana (Day 8): Remote setting, authentic mountain atmosphere—ideal last-night hut experience.

Book all rifugi months in advance, particularly from mid-July until August.

Access and Logistics

- Begin by taking a public bus or cab from Cortina d'Ampezzo or Dobbiaco station to Lago di Braies in Toblach.
- End: Belluno station, with trains and buses connecting to Venice, Milan, and Innsbruck.
- Transporting gear: Luggage transfer services exist but are limited—plan to carry your basics or use private transfer firms.
- Supply Stops: Minimal along route—Dobbiaco, Cortina, and a few villages accessible via short detours for supplies.

Why Does Alta Via 1 Matter?

Hiking Alta Via 1 is more than just a completed trail. It is a profound and significant meeting with the soul of the Dolomites itself. Each walk, every halt on the rifugi terraces, and each evening spent watching the alpenglow become a vivid chapter in memory.

By the end of their journey in Belluno's quiet streets, hikers realize something profound: this was never about speed, distance, or challenge alone, but rather the depth of experiences gathered along a route that was so perfectly balanced between wilderness and warmth, solitude and hospitality, silence and community.

Alta Via 1 is an invitation—an open door into a landscape where every turn reveals a fresh perspective, every rifugio provides shelter and warmth, and every summit whispers a narrative worth recounting for years.

Alta Via 2

Alta Via 2 isn't just another hike. It is an immersion into the Dolomites' most wild and dramatic shapes. Compared to the famed Alta Via 1, this path feels rawer, rougher, and unquestionably greater in scale. The landscape here talks loudly, revealing beautiful panoramas, quieter routes, and the joy of crossing challenging yet rewarding terrain.

This classic road runs approximately 160 kilometers from north to south, connecting the medieval alleys of Bressanone (Brixen) in South Tyrol to the historic town of Feltre in Veneto. It cuts through some of Italy's most dramatic landscape, including Puez-Odle's jagged spires, the lunar plateaus of the Sella group, the fortress-like massif of Marmolada—the Dolomites' highest peak—and the enigmatic Pale di San Martino range.

Alta Via 2 is more than just a trail; it's a story told in stone, meadow, ridge, and cloud, allowing the brave to engage in a deeper dialogue with nature's raw beauty.

Trail Overview and Route Details

- Starting Point: Bressanone (Brixen), South Tyrol
- End Point: Feltre, Veneto area.
- Length: About 160 kilometers (100 miles).
- Duration: Usually 10-13 days, depending on the speed and hut availability.
- Total elevation gain/loss: Approximately 10,000 meters of cumulative ascent/descent
- The highest point is 3,152 meters (Marmolada via optional detour), while the main route reaches around 2,950 meters at Passo delle Farangole.
- Difficulty: Challenging with some steep sections and significant daily ascent.
- Best Hiking Season: Early July to Mid-September

Sample Itinerary (Classic 11-Day Trek):

- Bressanone – Rifugio Plose (4-5 hours)
- Rifugio Plose-Rifugio Genova (Schlüterhütte) (6 hours)
- Rifugio Genova-Rifugio Puez (5-6 hours)

- Rifugio Puez - Passo Gardena - Rifugio Pisciadù (5 hours, difficult ascent assisted by ferrata)
- Rifugio Pisciadù-Rifugio Boè-Passo Pordoi (5-6 hours)
- Passo Pordoi – Rifugio Viel dal Pan – Rifugio Castiglioni Marmolada (6 hours)
- Rifugio Castiglioni-Rifugio Falier-Passo San Pellegrino (7-8 hours)
- Passo San Pellegrino – Rifugio Mulaz (6-7 hours)
- Rifugio Mulaz to Rifugio Rosetta (6 hours, difficult)
- Rifugio Rosetta-Rifugio Treviso (6 hours)
- Rifugio Treviso - Feltre (5-7 hour descent)

Each stage is carefully planned to strike a balance between challenge and comfort, with plenty of opportunity for introspection, photography, wildlife viewing, and cultural immersion in the rifugi.

Difficulty and Terrain Conditions

Alta Via 2 requires high physical condition and familiarity with alpine terrain. Unlike Alta Via 1, sections here may include steep ascents, loose scree, fixed cables (via ferrata sections), and exposed ridgelines.

- Trail surface: A combination of difficult mountain routes, steep scree slopes, some easy via ferrata with fixed ropes, and rocky terrain.
- Exposure and technicality: Moderate to high; some brief via ferrata or cable-secured sections.
- Weather considerations: Rapid weather changes are prevalent; storms and cold spells must be anticipated.

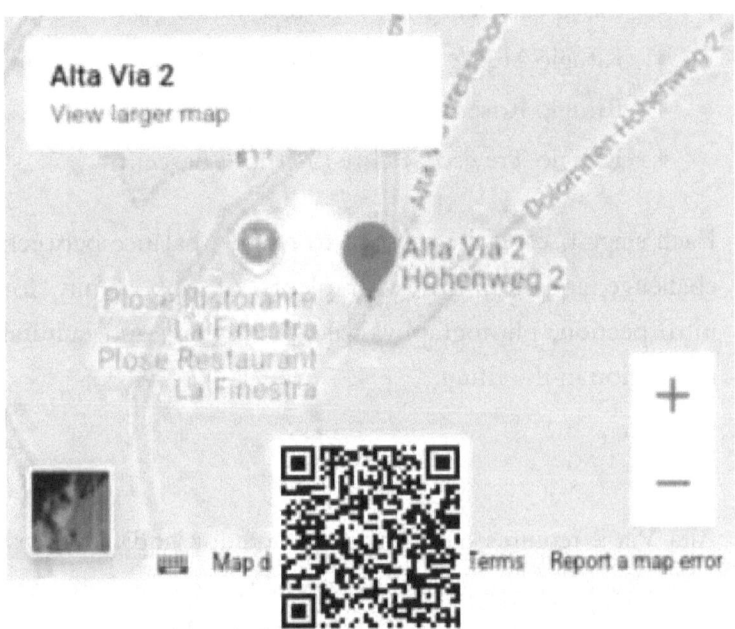

Scan for a **GPS-Enabled** Map Experience

Highlights and Viewpoints

Every day, Alta Via 2 weaves together dramatic, memorable highlights.

Panoramas of the Plose and Odle Groups, including iconic views from Rifugio Genova and the stunning Odle spires.

- The Puez Plateau is a vast, lunar landscape characterized by solitude.
- Sella Massif Traverse: Steep, rocky climbs with spectacular views and 360-degree panoramas.
- The Marmolada Massif offers breathtaking views of the Dolomites' greatest glacier and highest mountain.

Rifugio Rosetta offers breathtaking sunrises and sunsets on the Pale di San Martino Plateau.

Vette Feltrine Natural Park has less-explored, wild, and pristine areas with tremendous biodiversity.

Recommended Rifugi (Mountain Huts)

Alta Via 2's allure is based on these rifugi, strategically positioned refuges that provide hospitality, hearty meals, and mountain camaraderie:

- Rifugio Plose is a fantastic first-night stay, with beautiful views and friendly service.
- Rifugio Genova (Schlüterhütte): Delicious regional meals in a stunning location among the Odle mountains.
- Rifugio Puez: A remote, rural area ideal for starry sky and isolation.
- Rifugio Pisciadù: Perched beautifully, recognized for great meals and a welcoming setting.
- Rifugio Boè is the Sella Group's highest hut, with famous sunrises and panoramic mountain views.
- Rifugio Castiglioni Marmolada: A historic cabin beneath the glacier with excellent local cuisine.
- Rifugio Mulaz: Cozy, rustic, and hospitable; famous sunsets from the patio.
- Rifugio Rosetta: A high-altitude refuge with spectacular views of the Pale plateau.
- Treviso: Charming cabin with an original alpine environment and excellent welcome.
- Booking in advance is important, especially from mid-July to August.

Access & Logistics

- Bressanone is easily accessible by train from Innsbruck, Bolzano, and Verona.

- End destination: Feltre, with train connections to Venice, Padua, and beyond.
- Restock and gear transfers are limited; prepare to take only the essentials and restock at passes
- Safety precautions: Mountain rescue insurance is strongly advised. Weather conditions may influence daily stages.

Conclusion

Alta Via 2 is more than just a hike; it's a spectacular adventure into the Dolomites' wild core. From peaceful alpine valleys to dizzying passes, historic lodges to pristine wilderness, each step highlights the Dolomites' astounding diversity and raw beauty.

It's more than just finishing a path; it's about giving in to the power of these mountains. It's an experience defined not by distance but by moments of stillness before dawn, talks in small mountain cottages, and the quiet triumph felt at the top of each pass. Hikers depart Alta Via 2 feeling enriched, humbled, and deeply altered.

Seceda & Odle Group (Val Gardena)

The first moment at the peak ridge of Seceda is surreal. The terrain appears to give way, a grassy slope unraveling into a line of stone fangs—the Odle peaks—rising in a flawless, impossible row. It doesn't feel authentic. It's more like a scene prepared for something mythic.

This isn't just another picturesque hike in the Dolomites. Seceda and the Odle Group are examples of alpine experiences that stay with you for a long time. Everything about the site feels heightened—the light, the drama, the silence, and the ease with which the magnificent may be walked.

Seceda, located in Val Gardena, one of South Tyrol's most gorgeous and culturally rich valleys, is both accessible and immensely rewarding. From broad family-friendly day treks to magnificent ridge crossings and high-mountain hut excursions, this area provides some of the best value in the Dolomites. Casual hikers, seasoned trekkers, and photographers all come here to find the same thrill.

Where It Is and Why It Surprises

Seceda is located on the northwestern edge of the Puez-Odle Nature Park, which is part of the wider, UNESCO-listed Dolomites region. The spectacular spine of this area is formed by the Odle Group (Geislergruppe in German), which consists of slender, serrated limestone spires that rise to 3,000 meters.

Hikers can experience a surreal dual perspective thanks to the distinctive topography: soft alpine meadows rolling into the Sella and Sassolungo mountains to the south, and cliffs plummeting into forested valleys with the jagged Odle peaks forming an abrupt, vertical curtain to the north.

Scan for a GPS-Enabled Map Experience

It's a tremendously visual hike—every turn reveals a new aspect that appears to be built for a camera lens, but nothing feels staged. Nature at its most architectural.

Top Hiking Routes Around Seceda & the Odle Group

1. Seceda Summit Loop (Easy to Moderate)

- Route: Ortisei cable car, Seceda peak, Pieralongia, Rifugio Firenze, and return by Col Raiser.
- Loop distance: around 9 kilometers.
- Duration: 3-4 hours.
- Elevation gain: ~300 m (minimum when starting from lift).

This is the classic. Hikers enter an alpine amphitheatre when the cable car dumps them off at 2,500 meters. The path begins on the top ridge, a grassy, inclined plateau with the Odle range slashing the sky like stone knives.

The road then gently descends toward Pieralongia, a pair of unusual rock formations that serve as a natural pause spot. In July, wildflowers bloom along route borders, and marmots emerge from grassy burrows. It continues to Rifugio Firenze (Regensburger Hütte), an ideal lunch spot with views of the Sassolungo and Puez plateau.

Return via the Col Raiser cableway, or continue the hike via the forest and pastures.

2. Odle Panorama Trail (Family-friendly)

- Route: from Col Raiser station via Rifugio Firenze to Brogles Alm and back.
- Distance: Approximately 8 kilometers.
- Time: Three hours.
- Terrain: Gently sloping, with spacious trails and picnic-worthy spots.

Ideal for people looking for a relaxing day outdoors with breathtaking surroundings. Much of the trail is lined with larches, and wooden seats are placed at regular intervals, offering long rests with panoramic views. Ideal in late September, when larches turn gold and crowds thin off.

3. Rifugio to Rifugio Traverse (moderate to difficult)

- Route: Seceda, Rifugio Firenze, Rifugio Puez, Vallunga (exit in Selva).
- Distance: approximately 15 kilometers.
- Time: 6-7 hours.
- Recommended for full-day hikers and Alta Via 2 samplers.

A more ambitious route through the center of Puez-Odle Nature Park. This path begins in Seceda and climbs and dips across stony peaks and grassy saddles until it reaches the

Puez Plateau—a silent, fossil-rich region that feels more lunar than alpine. The drop into Vallunga returns you to the woodland and valley bottom. For those who do not complete Alta Via 2, this loop provides a generous sampling.

Difficulty Level

- Beginner to Moderate: Because of the lift-access trailheads and well-maintained pathways, most day hikes from Seceda or Col Raiser stations are suitable for beginners.
- Moderate to Strenuous: Longer hikes into Puez-Odle require endurance and confidence in rough terrain, but technical competence is rarely required.
- Altitude consideration: Starting at over 2,000 meters, even short climbs may feel exhausting at first. Acclimatization is beneficial.

Highlights and Natural Wonders

- Seceda Ridge is the region's famous, slanted ridgeline—a sweeping green shoulder that ends in an almost vertical cliff drop into Val di Funes.
- The Odle Group consists of bare limestone pinnacles that are often coated with snow, even in early summer, and are best observed from north-facing routes.
- Alpine Flora: From mid-June to July, fields of gentian, alpine aster, and fireweed bloom.

- Wildlife includes marmots, chamois, and golden eagles that soar overhead.
- Autumn Color: From mid-September until early October, larch woods blaze golden.

Access & Logistics

Primary access point: Ortisei (St. Ulrich) in Val Gardena.

Lifts:

- Seceda Cable Car (Ortisei-2,500m)
- Colonel Raiser Gondola (from Santa Cristina)

Best time to go:

- Late June to late September for full trail and rifugio access.
- September brings peace and fall colors.

Lift Schedule: Typically, from mid-June to early October; see the current year's schedule.

Recommended Refugi

- Rifugio Firenze / Regensburger Hütte: A classic on the Odle side, with superb meals, a magnificent patio, and easy access from both cableways.

- Rifugio Puez: Remote, sitting in the middle of the stone plateau—ideal for longer excursions and overnight stays.
- Brogles Alm: A calmer alpine chalet in a picturesque location above Val di Funes.
- Rifugio Juac: Located between Ortisei and Col Raiser, it's ideal for cake stops and sun-soaked lazing.

Booking overnight stays is strongly encouraged during busy seasons, particularly on weekends.

Conclusion

Some hikes are stunning with a single vista. Seceda delivers a dozen before lunchtime. However, it is not just about spectacle; it is also about how the landscape inspires reflection. The ridge provides a view of the entire world. The trails wind like stories through flowery fields and beneath towering stones, with only the occasional marmot breaking the silence.

Seiser Alm (Alpe di Siusi)

It is not necessarily the wildest landscapes that linger the longest; rather, it is those that provide breathing space.

Alpe di Siusi, also known as Seiser Alm in German, lacks spires and cliffs. It does not erupt into view like the Tre Cime or spiral upward like the Odle. Instead, it expands widely. The largest alpine meadow in Europe—spanning over 50 square kilometers—Alpe di Siusi unfolds like a sea of delicate gold and green, tucked beneath towering guardians Sciliar, Sassolungo, and Sassopiatto. The contrast is unsettling. Wildflowers bloom in gentle pastures, while vertical rock walls cast lengthy morning shadows. The cows graze. Cyclists pass by the chapel ruins. And what about the trails? They meander rather than ascend, allowing hikers the uncommon luxury of movement without tension, immersion without effort.

This is the Dolomites at their most tranquil.

Why does the Alpe di Siusi matter?

There are few places in the Alps that combine such vast landscape with such approachability. Seiser Alm is an ideal destination for day hikers, families, photographers, and those looking for a quieter alternative to the high passes and ridges.

It's a landscape that encourages slowing down.

- Gentle trails with spectacular views
- Floral diversity unparalleled in the region.
- Sunrise and sunset with wide-open skies
- Historical cabins, alpine farms, and culturally significant stops
- Ladin heritage is found in every nook of the region.

This is hardly the Dolomites of adventure and conquest. This is where they become poetic.

A Brief Overview of the Landscape

- Region: South Tyrol (Südtirol / Alto Adige).
- Part of: Sciliar-Catinaccio Nature Park.
- Elevation Range: 1,800-2,300 metres

- Surrounding Peaks: Sciliar (Schlern), Sassolungo (Langkofel), and Sassopiatto (Plattkofel).
- Area: Approximately 56 km²
- Languages include German, Ladin, and Italian.

Alpe di Siusi is surrounded by three large massifs and populated with rustic alpine lodges, old shepherd pathways, and scenic terraces. Even in July, the air is fresh and crisp. Wildflowers light up the slopes from June to early August, and in late September, the larch trees begin to blaze into gold.

Top Hiking Routes in the Alpe di Susi

1. Compaccio to Rifugio Bolzano (Moderate)

- Route: Compaccio-Saltnerhütte-Rifugio Bolzano-back
- The round-trip distance is around 13 kilometers.
- Time: 4-5 hours.
- Elevation gain: around 500 meters.

One of the few trails that leads to a real peak sense. The hike begins pleasantly across rolling pasture and then ascends through pine trees to the Schlern Plateau. Perched at 2,457 meters, Rifugio Bolzano offers breathtaking views across the South Tyrolean plains and back toward the Ortler Alps.

Ideal for day hikers looking for one of the region's top views.

2. Panorama Circuit: Easy to Moderate

- Route: From Compaccio to Hotel Icaro - Panorama Trail Loop - Compaccio
- Distance: around 9 kilometers.
- Duration: 2.5-3 hours.
- Elevation gain: approximately 200 meters.

Scan for a GPS-Enabled Map Experience

Seiser Alm's soul is vast, kind, and always scenic. Trails wind through flower-filled meadows, providing views of Sassolungo at all times. Wooden chairs arise at ideal intervals, while huts such as Gostner Schwaige entice with homemade cheese dumplings and fresh elderflower spritz.

3. Saltria to Monte Pana and back (family-friendly)

- Saltria, Monte Pana, and back to Saltria.
- Distance: Approximately 7 kilometers.
- Duration: 2 hours.
- Highlights: playground stops, cable car option return, picnic places.

A pleasant stroll ideal for toddlers and multigenerational groups. Along the road, there are tranquil pastures, little chapels, and woodland margins that are shadowed. It's the type of path where everyone finds their groove—without tiredness.

4. Sassolungo Circuit (Strenuous)

- Route: From Passo Sella to Rifugio Toni Demetz - complete loop around Sassolungo.
- Distance: Approximately 17 kilometers.
- Time: 6-7 hours.
- Elevation Gain: Approximately 750 meters

This trail technically located on the outskirts of Seiser Alm, however it connects immediately through lifts or connecting trails. For fit hikers, the circuit around Sassolungo and Sassopiatto provides a true alpine challenge, with towering walls, scree-filled passes, and peaceful valleys framed by giants. Rifugi along the way break up the climb, making it manageable as a day loop or a two-day overnight.

Highlights & Natural Beauty

- Sunrises at Compaccio: Golden hour illuminates the field like a painting.
- The Sciliar Plateau is a stark and silent limestone table on the edge of the globe.
- Alpine flora: From late June to early August, orchids, wild arnica, gentian, and thyme blossom in large numbers.
- Pasture culture: Watch alpine cows graze beneath Sassolungo, their bells booming across the vast terrain.
- Rifugi cuisine: Order the Kaiserschmarrn at the Rifugi. Accept the recommendation.

Access & Logistics

Base villages:

- Ortisei (St. Ulrich): greatest all-around hub
- Castelrotto (Kastelruth) - lovely and peaceful

- Siusi allo Sciliar (Seis am Schlern) - accessible via gondola

Public Transportation:

- Cable cars from Ortisei and Siusi (seasonal).
- Shuttle buses from the Alpe di Siusi Station at Castelrotto

Car access restrictions:

- From 9:00 a.m. Private vehicles are not allowed to enter Seiser Alm until 5 p.m. Arrive early or use the lift/shuttle system.

Best time to visit:

- Trails, lifts, and Rifugi are open from late June to early October.
- Mid-July: peak wildflower season
- Mid-September - the larch season begins, and trails become quiet.

Recommended Rifugi & Stops

- Gostner Schwaige is a gourmet pasture hut. Hay-infused milk, alpine cheese plates, and handcrafted pastries are all popular.

- Rifugio Bolzano: Located on a stark high plateau with amazing vistas and a true summit experience.
- Rifugio Molignon is a pleasant location for an overnight stay or a mid-hike meal, nestled in a secluded meadow.
- Rifugio Alpe di Tires: Located halfway between Seiser Alm and the Rosengarten, it is suitable for hut-to-hut links.

Conclusion

It's all about contrast. The intimacy of cow trails underfoot, the immensity of cliffs above. The smell of grass warming up in the sun. The silence was immense and constant, interrupted only by wind and bells. And the gradual draw of a trail that never rushes, but always leads to a worthwhile destination.

Seiser Alm does not make demands. It is welcoming. In doing so, it provides one of the most relaxing and magnificent hiking experiences in the Dolomites. There's no mountain to climb here, only a sense that you've landed exactly where you should be.

Sassolungo and Sassopiatto

The Sassolungo (Langkofel) and Sassopiatto (Plattkofel) massifs are one of the Dolomites' most dominating duos, combining sheer vertical drama with broad, walking openness. Standing shoulder to shoulder between Val Gardena and Val di Fassa, they rise like sculpted sentinels, surrounded by flowering meadows, stone pathways, scree valleys, and windswept high passes.

Hiking around them is more than simply a path; it's an entire orbit. The Sassolungo/Sassopiatto loop is one of the most full single-day hikes in the Dolomites: panoramic, emotional, physically demanding, and punctuated by moments of majesty that last long after the boots are removed.

Why Hike Here?

Few other circuits can match this one's rhythm. The sheer enormity of Sassolungo's face gives way to a surprising intimacy as the trail wraps around it—passes open unexpectedly, glacial valleys appear with echoes of water, and the ridge between Sassopiatto and Alpe di Siusi stretches wide enough for thinking to breathe.

Nonetheless, it's approachable. This hard but achievable loop, complete with strategically placed cable cars and rifugi, appeals to everyone from seasoned trekkers to strong-spirited day hikers. There is no better orbit for individuals looking to immerse themselves in a truly Dolomitic universe of scale, light, and silence.

The mountains themselves

Sassolungo (Langkofel)

- Elevation: 3,181m
- Profile: narrow, jagged, vertical.
- Highlights include the sheer north face seen from Val Gardena, deep-cut cirques, and the stunning saddle pass.

Sassopiatto (Plattkofel)

- Elevation: 2,964 meters.
- Profile: Rounded summit with a lengthy ridgeline
- Highlights: Wide plateau vistas, rolling scree fields, and moderate eastern slopes over Alpe di Siusi.

They form a bookend shape on the skyline. One sharp and unyielding. The other is broad-shouldered and open to the sun.

Hiking Overview: The Full Circuit

Sassolungo & Sassopiatto Loop Trail.

- Route: Passo Sella, Rifugio Toni Demetz, Rifugio Vicenza, Rifugio Sassopiatto, Rifugio Comici, and back to Passo Sella.
- Loop distance: around 17 km.

- Time: 6 to 7 hours, barring long pauses.
- Elevation gain/loss: around 600-800 meters.
- Trail markers: Mostly CAI trails 525, 527, 528, and 526.

It's a full-circle route that takes you through alpine basins, steep climbs, scree-filled passages, and panoramic grassland terraces. The trail climbs from Passo Sella into the small cleft beneath Sassolungo, where Rifugio Toni Demetz (2,685 m) sits like an outpost in the sky.

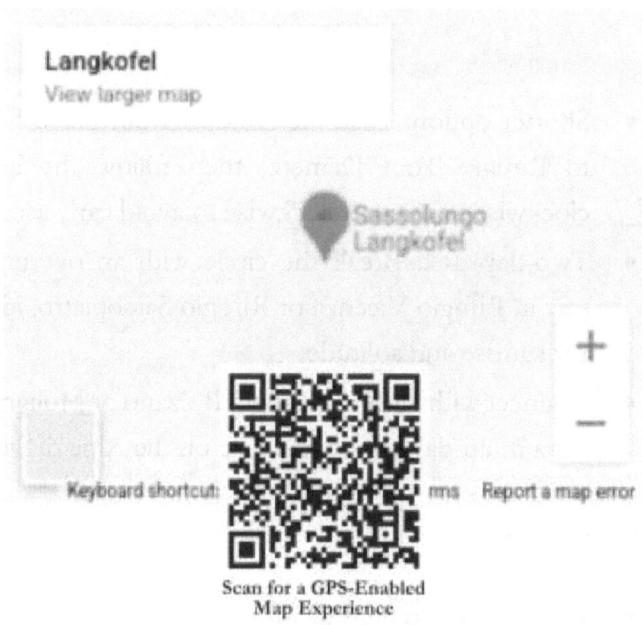

Scan for a GPS-Enabled Map Experience

The descent into the Valle dei Sassolungo exposes a glacial-shaped bowl of stillness and stone, leading to Rifugio Vicenza, nestled in the shade of the cliffs. Stone walls at this location feel close, protecting, and enormous.

The second half of the hike takes you into more open landscape. Rifugio Sassopiatto sits on a natural shelf with a breathtaking view of the Catinaccio and Latemar groups. Beyond that, the landscape gradually slopes into Alpe di Siusi before returning to Rifugio Comici, a gourmet refuge and the loop's final high point.

Alternative Routes and Variations

- Shorter option: Take the gondola from Passo Sella to Rifugio Toni Demetz, then follow the loop clockwise or counterclockwise to avoid early ascent.
- Two-day trek: Break the circle with an overnight stay in Rifugio Vicenza or Rifugio Sassopiatto, ideal for sunrise and solitude.
- Connect with paths to Rifugio Bolzano or Molignon for a multi-day hut-to-hut hike on the Alpe di Siusi.

Difficulty level

- Fitness level required: Moderate to strong hiking stamina. The trail is not challenging, but the entire

loop has extended spells of no shade and steady elevation change.
- There is little need for via ferrata gear, but proper boots, poles, and weatherproof clothing are required.
- Weather alert: An early start is recommended. Thunderstorms in the afternoon can suddenly sweep across the Sassolungo saddle.

Highlights from the Trail

- Rifugio Toni Demetz: Located in a narrow saddle, it feels like a lunar station above the globe.
- Rifugio Vicenza (Langkofelhütte): One of the most atmospheric huts in the Dolomites, located near high cliffs.
- Views from the Sassopiatto ridge include an infinite view east across the Alpe di Siusi and the Sciliar Massif.
- Rifugio Comici: Elegant, panoramic, and renowned for its excellent cuisine—ideal for a leisurely meal or concluding toast.
- Chamois, marmots, and golden eagles were spotted overhead.
- Best lighting for photography: Early dawn (counter-clockwise start) or late afternoon (clockwise).

Access & Logistics

Trailhead: Passo Sella (2,218 m).

- Selva di Val Gardena, Canazei, and Ortisei may all be reached by vehicle or public shuttle.
- Parking is limited; arrive early in the summer months.

Cable cars:

- Forcella del Sassolungo lift: A small gondola (standing only) connects Passo Sella and Toni Demetz, providing an incredible vertical ascent through a rock gorge. It operates from late June to late September.

The best months:

- All huts are open from late June to late September, and the route is snow-free.
- Mid-September: Perfect for golden light, deserted trails, and peaceful rifugi.

Recommended Refugi

- Rifugio Toni Demetz: One of the tallest huts in the region, basic but remarkable in its setting.

- Rifugio Vicenza offers rustic charm, excellent traditional Ladin cuisine, and the kind of calm that only stone walls can provide.
- Rifugio Sassopiatto: Warm environment, large terrace, ideal for overnight stays.
- Rifugio Comici: Upscale alpine dining recognized for its inventive South Tyrolean meals and stunning wine list.

In peak season, book overnight shelters at least 6-8 weeks ahead of time.

Tips:

Clockwise vs. Counterclockwise:

- Clockwise: Early ascent is longer, but the descent is softer, making it excellent for the golden hour return.
- Counter-clockwise: Easiest on knees, popular with photographers seeking early light on Sassopiatto.

Hydration is essential: carry at least 2L. Refill at the rifugi or alpine springs.

Storms move quickly, so pack layers and monitor the sky after lunchtime.

Consider extending: Spend a night in Alpe di Siusi or combine with Rosengarten for a multi-day Dolomite adventure.

To close, few trails convey the entire personality of the Dolomites as well as this one. The Sassolungo/Sassopiatto circuit is an alpine symphony, with narrow valleys, wide-open meadows, scree-strewn ridges, and pine-scented slopes. It's magnificent and humble. Strenuous but meditative. The scale shifts from familiar to foreign.

The trail winds its way through wildflowers at times. Next, it's skirting beneath a 3,000-meter steep limestone wall. It's like journeying through the heart of something ancient, and coming out the other side with a better understanding of what it means to be a part of it.

Cinque Torri & Lagazuoi

Cinque Torri—a cluster of stone towers rising like old fingers from the earth—is located in the heart of the Ampezzo Dolomites, directly above Cortina d'Ampezzo. A few ridgelines away, the enormous plateau of Lagazuoi spreads beneath the heavens, pierced by military tunnels and dotted with views so expansive that they leave you speechless.

Cinque Torri and Lagazuoi provide more than simply some of the best mid-altitude trekking in the Dolomites. This is a location where beauty and history are inextricably linked, where wildflower pathways go through trenches, and sunrises show not just craggy peaks, but the ghosts of a mountain war that once shook the stone.

Why hike here?

Few hiking sites in the Dolomites compress so much scenic drama, accessibility, and historical significance into such a small, walkable region. Meadows to rock, wartime trenches to panoramic decks, scree slopes to peaceful lakes—the landscape changes quickly. Nonetheless, it remains one of the most accessible areas, ideal for strenuous day hikes, family outings, and history-rich detours.

Highlights?

- Extraordinary views with minimal climb.
- WWI open-air museums built into the cliffs
- High-altitude rifugio with cable car access.
- Access to extended hut-to-hut expansions or Alta Via connections.
- Late-season beauty—one of the few places that October still works.

It is more than just a spot to hike. It's a spot worth remembering.

Trail Overview: Main Routes in the Area

1. Cinque Torri Loop and Open-Air WWI Museum (Easy to Moderate)

- Route: Rifugio Scoiattoli, WWI Trenches, around the towers, Rifugio Cinque Torri
- Distance: approximately 4.5 kilometers.
- Time: 1.5 to 2 hours
- Elevation gain: approximately 150 m.

This loop is a great way to get to know the area and is both fun for the kids and rather absorbing. Begin at Rifugio

Scoiattoli, where the towers immediately draw notice. The walk leads through an open-air museum, where rebuilt WWI trenches, artillery positions, and information boards recount the narrative of Italian and Austro-Hungarian troops battling not only one another, but also the mountain.

Walk through history, then follow peaceful trails that circle the stone spires. The stark contrast between the tranquil meadow environment and the horrific past beneath your boots is remarkable.

2. Lagazuoi WWI Tunnel Descent (Moderate; tricky in portions)

- Route: Lagazuoi cable car station, peak, Kaiserjäger route, or Via del Tunnel, Passo Falzarego.
- Distance: around 7 km round trip or 5 km one-way.
- Time: 3–4 hours
- Elevation loss: approximately 600 m.

This is the Dolomites at their most haunting. After taking the Lagazuoi cable car to 2,752 meters, begin at Rifugio Lagazuoi and descend down the Via del Tunnel, a wartime tunnel built right through the mountain. The tunnel is dark, cold, wet, and extremely gripping—headlamps are required, as are thick footwear and caution on the slick rock.

The tunnel emerges into switchbacks that lead back to Passo Falzarego. This is not a hike to forget. It is not intended to be.

3. Cinque Torri to Lagazuoi Traverse (full-day hike)

- Route: Rifugio Scoiattoli, Forcella Averau, Rifugio Lagazuoi, e Passo Falzarego.
- Distance: around 12 kilometers.
- Time: 6–7 hours
- Elevation gain: ~600 meters

A breathtaking day trek that connects both landmarks in one wonderful circuit. Climb softly from the towers to Forcella Averau, then skirt the ridge beyond Rifugio Averau and Rifugio Nuvolau (the sunset here is magnificent). Continue across wild, open terrain to Rifugio Lagazuoi, which offers views of the Marmolada, Tofane, and even Austria on a clear day.

Descend via the tunnel or the Kaiserjäger trail, which is more open and scenic, with less risks.

Difficulty levels

- Cinque Torri Loop: Easy to moderate—great for first-time Dolomite hikers, families, and history enthusiasts.

- Lagazuoi descent: Moderate with technical footing; headlamps and caution required.
- Full traverse: Moderate to difficult, depending on pace; exposure at some sections, but no technical equipment required.

The entire area is located between 2,000 and 2,800 meters, thus the weather changes quickly. Early starts and layers are not optional.

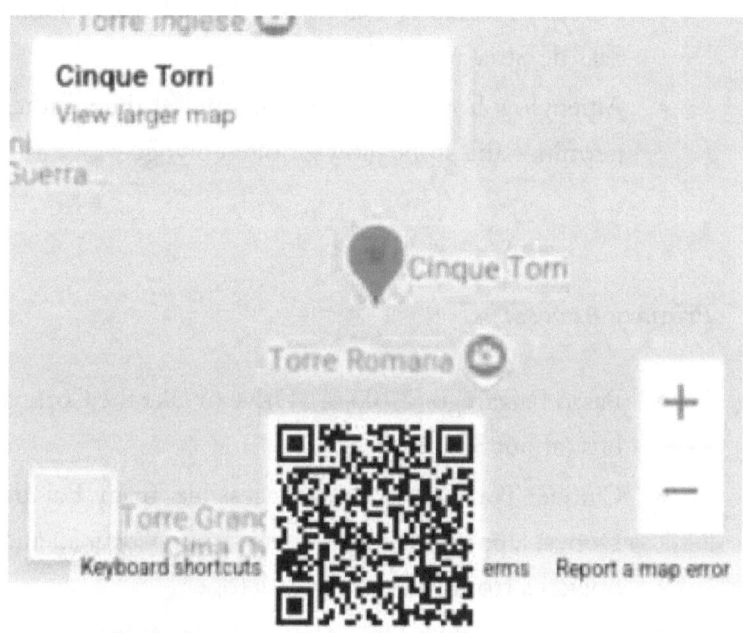

Scan for a GPS-Enabled Map Experience

Highlights & Viewpoints

- Rifugio Scoiattoli deck: A classic Dolomite view of Cinque Torri from eye level.
- Rifugio Lagazuoi terrace: Possibly the most panoramic point in the region—the dawn and sunset illuminate the entire range.
- WWI trenches and galleries: walkable, depressing, and remarkably conserved.
- Forcella Averau is a dramatic ridge that overlooks Sass de Stria and Tofane.
- Alpenglow hours: Stay until nightfall if the weather permits—the stone glows molten orange.

Access and Logistics

Primary Access:

- Passo Falzarego (2,105 m): Drive or take the Cortina bus (about 30 minutes).
- Cinque Torri Chairlift is accessible from Bai de Dones, approximately 10 km from Cortina, and operates from June to early October.
- Lagazuoi Cable Car: From Passo Falzarego to Rifugio Lagazuoi—open from mid-June to early October.

Trail signage: Clear CAI markings throughout (routes 439, 440, 412, and 402 are important).

Best months:

- Late June to late September for full-service huts and museum admission.
- Early October for pure air, empty routes, and burning larches (confirm lift operation dates).

Recommended Rifugi

- Rifugio Scoiattoli is located at the foot of Cinque Torri and is ideal for lunch, cake, or an overnight stay with a view of the mountains.
- Rifugio Averau: Small but excellent meals; a great halfway point for lengthy treks.
- Rifugio Nuvolau: Perched alone on a hilltop with breathtaking 360° views. Worth the climb.
- Rifugio Lagazuoi is legendary. Basic, but memorable. Sunsets in this area are very unforgettable.

These cottages are popular for a reason, so book ahead of time during peak season.

Insider Tips

- Bring a headlamp: the WWI tunnel path is unlit, and natural light fades quickly underneath.
- Sunset strategy: Stay overnight at Rifugio Lagazuoi or schedule a late-day lift for golden hour magnificence.
- Educational depth: The open-air museum signage is bilingual and carefully managed. Take time to read.
- Link with Alta Via 1: This portion is part of the Alta Via 1 and is an excellent addition to any longer hut-to-hut trip.

Conclusion

Beauty here is not limited to the summits. It's in the stories they've kept for more than a century. Cinque Torri's sheer vertical towers, Lagazuoi's windswept silence, and the delicate balance of natural majesty and human memory all come together in a sweeping scene.

This is a trip through light and stone, as well as through history. A spot where footsteps reverberate over millennia. Where every viewpoint incorporates the past. And where every trace, no matter how gentle, has the weight of something once fiercely battled for.

Rosengarten/Catinaccio Group

The Rosengarten, also known as Catinaccio in Italian, rises between Val di Fassa and Val d'Ega, forming a towering procession of dolomitic spires immortalized in Ladin tradition. It's here that King Laurin's enchanted rose garden is fabled to blossom, and where the mountains still glow crimson at sunset, long after the last footsteps have stopped on the trails.

But don't be mistaken: this range isn't all poetry and legends. The Rosengarten/Catinaccio is raw Dolomitic beauty: jagged, carved, imposing, and completely captivating. Trails lead through silent high valleys, across bare stone saddles, along knife-edge slopes, and into wildflower-filled alpine bowls surrounded by thousand-foot cliffs. The landscape changes dramatically—technical one moment, pastoral the next.

Hiking here seems like following a plot carved in stone, with the light changing the script by the hour.

Where It Is and Why It Captivates

The Rosengarten massif runs between Bolzano to the west and Canazei to the east, rising like a fortress wall above Vigo di Fassa, Tires, and Nova Levante. It is a central component of the Sciliar-Catinaccio Nature Park, and while it is generally less crowded than Seceda or Tre Cime, it contains some of the Dolomites' most varied and intimate alpine terrain.

- North: Craggy towers surround the Vajolet Valley and Rifugio Re Alberto.
- South: the spectacular Antermoia Basin and its glacier-fed lake.
- West: Forested slopes rising from Val d'Ega to Rifugio Fronza alle Coronelle.
- East: Open vistas down towards Val di Fassa and connects to Passo Principe.

The area is tight, self-contained, and extremely diverse—a hiker's paradise with a mythical backdrop.

Best Hiking Routes in the Rosengarten Group

1. Vajolet Towers Trail (moderate to strenuous)

- Route: from Rifugio Gardeccia to Rifugio Vajolet to Rifugio Re Alberto I and back.
- Distance: approximately 9 kilometers round trip.
- Time: 4–5 hours
- Elevation gain: approximately 750 m.
- Starting point: take the cable car to Ciampedie and then climb into the Gardeccia Valley.

Scan for a GPS-Enabled Map Experience

The centerpiece. This path takes you straight into the heart of the massif, rising through stone passageways to the towering Torri del Vajolet—six slim, vertical pinnacles that look like something out of a mountaineer's fever dream. The final portion to Rifugio Re Alberto I is steep, rocky, and thrilling, with chains in some places. What's the reward? One of the most dramatic mountain views in the Dolomites.

2. Rifugio Antermoia via Passo Principe (Challenging)

Rifugio Vajolet, Passo Principe, Rifugio Antermoia, Lago d'Antermoia, and return by Passo Ciaregole.

- Distance: around 14 kilometers.
- Time: 6–7 hours
- Elevation gain: approximately 900 m.
- Highlights include Alpine moonscapes, glacial lakes, and lonely alpine valleys.

A journey into the quieter heart of the Rosengarten. After ascending through scree and switchbacks to Passo Principe, the trail turns into lunar terrain. Rifugio Antermoia appears as a mirage above a stone amphitheater. The turquoise lake next to it, Lake d'Antermoia, sits at 2,495 meters and is wind-chilled and captivating.

3. Coronelle Pass Loop (moderate)

- Route: From Rifugio Fronza to Passo delle Coronelle - Tschafon - return
- Distance: around 10 kilometers.
- Time: 4–5 hours
- Trail type: Loop with one tough ascent over the pass.

This loop is ideal for hikers based in Tires or Nova Levante, providing spectacular views of the western Dolomites. The trail begins at the rifugio and ascends a rough pass before opening into a large alpine bowl. The path is quieter than the Vajolet corridor, with lengthy stretches of seclusion and varied topography.

4. Rifugio to Rifugio Traverse (Strenuous, Multi-Day Option)

- Route: Rifugio Fronza, Rifugio Roda di Vael, Rifugio Vajolet, Rifugio Passo Principe, and Rifugio Antermoia.
- Distance: around 25+ kilometers over 2-3 days.
- Ideal for: Hikers looking to immerse themselves in hut culture and explore the entire massif.

Connects various significant sites with an immersive hut-to-hut tour. Bunks, warm dinners, morning light, and the cadence of stone and footsteps—this is a Rosengarten trip. Can be expanded or shortened according to preference.

Difficulty Levels

- Moderate to strenuous: Most routes feature steep climbs, rocky switchbacks, and alternative via ferrata variations.
- There is no technical climbing necessary, although sure footing is essential, particularly above Vajolet and on high passes such as Principe and Ciaregole.

- Ideal for: Fit hikers with some alpine experience. Children older than ten will enjoy easier segments such as Ciampedie to Rifugio Gardeccia.

Highlights & Viewpoints

- Torri del Vajolet: Undisputed crown jewels, best seen at daybreak or early sunset.
- Lago di Antermoia: Quiet, windswept, glacier blue, and almost spiritual in its surroundings.
- Rifugio Passo Principe: Hidden in stone, like a mountain monk's retreat.
- Ciampedie Plateau: An excellent base for families—picnic areas, moderate trails, and panoramic benches.

Access and Logistics

Major access points:

- Vigo di Fassa (Cable vehicle to Ciampedie)
- Tires / Tiers (shuttle to Frommer Alm and lift to Rifugio Fronza)
- Nova Levante/Welschnofen (cable car to Laurin I and II)

Trail signage: Well-marked CAI signs, multilingual (German/Italian), with several Ladin place names.

Best months:

- Late June until mid-October.
- Full rifugi operation and snow-free passes are available from mid-July to late September.

Recommended Rifugi

- Rifugio Re Alberto I: Located just beneath the Vajolet Towers—basic beds, powerful location.
- Rifugio Vajolet: Well-run, friendly, excellent cuisine, and suitable for an overnight stay before Passo Principe.
- Rifugio Antermoia offers modern luxury in a dreamlike setting; don't miss the nearby lake.
- Rifugio Passo Principe is remote and small, but it makes up for it with closeness and tranquility.
- Rifugio Roda di Vael: Great meals and views of Catinaccio's southern reaches.

Advance reservations are required in July and August.

Insider Tips

- Start early: The morning light on the Vajolet Towers is memorable, and the trails are calmer.
- Sunset enthusiasts should spend the night at Re Alberto or Antermoia to witness the alpenglow paint the peaks.

- Try the canederli (bread dumplings) and the spiral fritters.
- For solitude, go in mid-September—crisp air, fewer people, and burning larches.

Conclusion

Certain Dolomites require respect. These evoke reverence. The Rosengarten/Catinaccio massif provides more than simply views; it also offers presence. One can sense the weight of time here. In the silence of stone valleys, in the breeze off Passo Principe, and in the flickering light that reflects off the Vajolet towers at sunset.

And when the alpenglow hits—enrosadira, that haunting Ladin pink—you realize why legends were born here. It's not a myth. It's memory, preserved in rock and light.

Pale di San Martino

It begins as a forest. Soft trees groan in the wind, accompanied by cowbells and the faint rush of high-altitude streams. But keep walking, keep climbing, and the world will fade away. Suddenly, the trees vanish, and the trail opens into a vast, pallid void. A desert of stones. A high elevation plateau floating in the sky. Welcome to the Pale di San Martino, the most strange and solitary hiking destination in the Dolomites.

Here, it no longer feels like Italy. It does not even feel like the Alps. It feels like you're wandering on another planet.

Why hike the Pale di San Martino?

Of all the Dolomite massifs, the Pale is the most mysterious. The largest group by surface area, but perhaps the least understood. Hikers come here for silence, scale, and solitude, not to go rifugi hopping or take classic photographs. This is the place to go when you need some space around your ideas or if you want to vanish into high mountain stillness for a day or three.

But there is no lack of drama. With alpine arrogance, peaks like Cimon della Pala—nicknamed "the Matterhorn of the Dolomites"—cut into the skies. The Altiplano delle Pale, a vast plateau spanning 50 square kilometers and rising to 2,500 meters, feels more at home in Iceland than in northern Italy. And the Paneveggio Forest, famous for its violin wood, hums with life just beneath.

Where It is

The Pale di San Martino is located in the Trentino region and is part of the Paneveggio-Pale di San Martino Natural Park, close above the lovely hamlet of San Martino di Castrozza. The massif borders the Veneto region to the east and is part of the Dolomiti Bellunesi UNESCO World Heritage Site.

Unlike the more heavily frequented northern ranges, this section of the Dolomites remains relatively quiet, even during peak season.

Top Hiking Routes in the Pale of San Martino

1. Altiplano delle Pale Circuit (moderate to strenuous)

- Route: Colverde cable car, Rifugio Rosetta, Altiplano loop, return.

- Distance: around 10-14 km (loop varies)
- Time: 5–7 hours
- Elevation gain/loss: ~600 meters
- Terrain: High plateau, rocky, and frequently trailless in appearance

This is the center of the Pale. After a quick lift ride from San Martino to Rifugio Rosetta, the trail leads to an eerie, lunar landscape. Cairns and red-white CAI markings help with wayfinding, but the overall impression is one of complete remoteness. Just rock, sky, and a repetitive crunch underfoot.

The circuit can be modified—short loops at Passo Pradidali Basso, or longer variants that reach Passo Canali and return. Expect scree, loneliness, and vastness. Snowfields may last far into July.

2. Rifugio Rosetta to Rifugio Pradidali Traverse (Strenuous)

- Route: Rifugio Rosetta, Passo di Ball, Rifugio Pradidali, return or descend.
- Distance: around 12 kilometers.
- Time: 6–7 hours
- Highlights include narrow ledges, precipitous plunges, and large south-facing cliffs.

A thrilling journey around the Pale's southern cliffs. Passo di Ball leads to a world of towers and shadows. The descent into Rifugio Pradidali is framed by stone amphitheaters with mythological proportions. Not recommended for people afraid of heights, but unforgettable for those who dare it.

There is also the option of staying overnight in Pradidali and returning the next day via Val Canali.

Scan for a GPS-Enabled Map Experience

3. Cimon della Pala Lookout (Easy-moderate)

- Route: From Passo Rolle via Capanna Cervino to Baita Segantini.
- Distance: around 6 kilometers round trip.
- Duration: 2-3 hours.
- Ideal for families, photographers, and golden hour views.

This is the Dolomites as a postcard fantasy. A short yet worthwhile trek leads to one of the Pale's most popular photo sites. Baita Segantini, situated by a tiny lake, perfectly frames Cimon della Pala in reflection. The best time to visit is early in the morning or at dusk, when the peaks blaze rose and orange.

4. Multi-Day Traverse: Pale Crossing

- Route: San Martino, Rosetta, Pradidali, Canali, and Passo Cereda.
- Duration: 3–4 days
- Overnights at Rifugio Rosetta, Rifugio Pradidali, and Rifugio Treviso.

A true Dolomite wilderness hike. This point-to-point path winds through the Pale's stone labyrinth, remaining high and remote before plunging into the thick woodland at Passo

Cereda. It's for hikers who want to experience the entire weight and wonder of the Pale, one hut at a time.

Difficulty Levels

- Moderate to strenuous: Trails are frequently unshaded, rocky, and require confidence on uneven terrain. Some trails traverse narrow cliffs or exposed saddles.
- No technical climbing, but some routes include steep drop-offs and scree. Trekking poles are advised.
- Altitude: Most routes operate above 2,200 meters—acclimatization is beneficial.

Access and Logistics

Base Town: San Martino di Castrozza.

- Quiet, alpine, well-equipped with shops, hotels, and equipment rentals.
- Regional buses connect Trento and Belluno.

Lifts:

- Colverde / Rosetta cable vehicle operates from mid-June until late September.

- Passo Rolle shuttle: summer only, links to numerous trailheads.

Best Season:

- Early July through late September
- Snowfields may remain on the plateau till late June.
- Early October delivers golden larches and cold clarity.

Recommended Rifugi.

- The Pale plateau's primary entryway is Rifugio Rosetta. High, airy, and inviting. Make an advance booking.
- Rifugio Pradidali: Nestled deep among a stony cirque. One of the most atmospheric cabins in the area.
- Rifugio Treviso: Forested and peaceful, the ideal concluding point for southerly treks.
- Baita Segantini is not a rifugio, but rather a magnificent day stop with one of the nicest views of the Dolomites.

Highlights and Visual Moments

- Sunrise on the plateau: The shadows stretch forever. Colors change by the second.

- Baita Segantini reflection shot: A Dolomites classic that is still worth every click.
- Sheer silence: On the Altiplano, silence comes alive.
- The barriers between Rosetta and Pradidali seem to go on forever.
- Violin trees below: The Paneveggio Forest grows the wood for Stradivari's violins, adding another element to the story.

Insider Tips

- Don't rush: The Pale focuses on absorption rather than destination. Take your time on the plateau, soaking in the solitude.
- Keep an eye on the weather: On the Altiplano, afternoon storms hit quickly and hard. Begin early.
- Stay high: Spend a night at Rosetta or Pradidali to truly experience seclusion over 2,500 meters.
- Bring a compass or GPS because the trails on the plateau can be difficult to see in the fog. Be aware of your bearings.

Conclusion

Hiking the Pale di San Martino is not about peak-bagging or rifugio hopping. It is about space. Vast, disturbing, and clarifying space. It's about traveling under towers that dwarf the imagination, into hallways of silence where the mind eventually stops clattering.

When the wind dies down and the sunshine slants exactly right on the pale stone, the world appears less crowded. There is now more space in the Pale. Room to move, think, and simply exist in a landscape large enough to accommodate it all.

Fanes-Sennes-Braies Natural Park

Some spots in the Dolomites unfold like outdoor theaters. Others, such as Fanes-Sennes-Braies, feel sacred, quiet, historic, and rooted in something older than time. The tale of the old Ladin Kingdom of Fanes still whispers across the valleys, where marmots outnumber humans, and alpine plateaus so vast that you can't hear your footsteps.

The park spans over 25,000 hectares and connects Val Badia, Val Pusteria, and Cortina d'Ampezzo, weaving together virgin meadows, lunar plateaus, mirrored lakes, and densely forested corridors. Here, Dolomite drama meets nature tranquility. The terrain is generous but humble. It encourages solitude and rewards curiosity.

Why hike here?

For those who desire the outdoors without compromising beauty or culture, this park provides the ideal balance:

- Expansive plateaus enabled multi-day exploration.
- Iconic alpine lakes, especially the jewel-toned Lake of Braies
- Easier elevation climbs than other places, but equal visual payoff.
- Remote rifugi hidden among valleys inaccessible by road.
- Ladin tradition is embedded into every cottage, landmark, and legend.

This is not the Dolomites as a spectacle. This is the Dolomites' presence: huge, silent, and unforgettable.

Where It Is and What It Includes

Fanes-Sennes-Braies Nature Park is located in South Tyrol, near the Veneto border to the east and wedged between two major Dolomite basins: Alta Badia to the south and Dobbiaco/Braies to the north.

The park is naturally separated into three main sectors:

- Fanes Plateau (south): A karstic plateau with a fairytale network of rifugi and pathways.
- Sennes Plateau (central): Wild grassy highlands surrounded by quiet.

- Braies Valley (north): Home to the renowned Lago di Braies, thick woodlands, and family-friendly pathways.

Top Hiking Routes in the Park

1. Lago di Braies Circuit + Val di Foresta (easy to moderate)

- Route: Loop around the lake + extension into Val di Foresta.
- Distance: around 6-8 kilometers.
- Duration: 2-3 hours.
- Ideal for: Photographers, families, and early risers.

Start early to ensure you get the lake to yourself. The 3.5-kilometer loop around Lago di Braies is flat, beautiful, and legendary for good reason. Continue to Val di Foresta, a quieter stretch where crowds decrease and trees absorb noise.

Best at dawn, when the mirror-like river reflects Croda del Becco in complete calm.

2. Rifugio Fanes and Lavarella from Pederü (Moderate)

- Route: Pederü, Rifugio Fanes, Rifugio Lavarella, and return.

- Distance: approximately 13 kilometers round trip.
- Time: 4–5 hours
- Elevation gain: ~600 meters

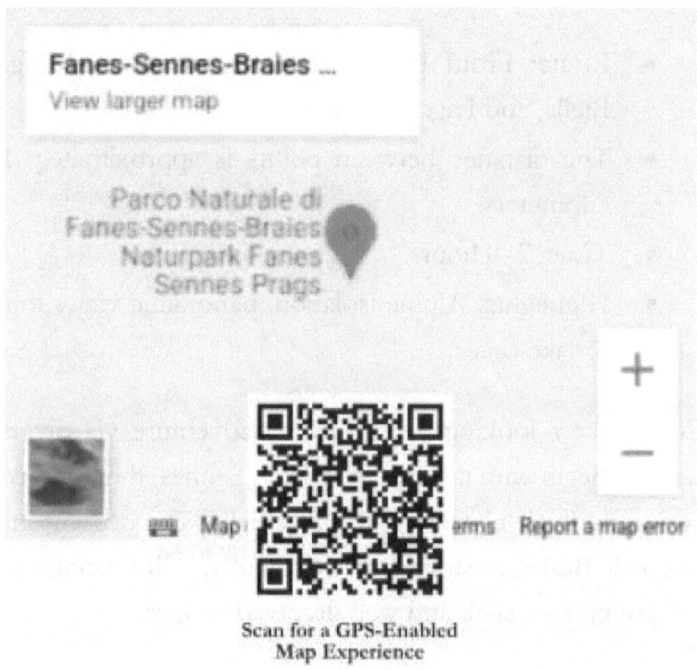

Scan for a GPS-Enabled Map Experience

The quintessential Fanes experience. Starting from Pederü, a steep jeep path leads into the vast Fanes plateau. There, Rifugio Fanes and Rifugio Lavarella await, inviting outposts of Ladin hospitality. The surrounding terrain appears large and open, with expansive views, grassy hollows, and hidden lakes.

Ideal for an overnight stay with sunrise excursions to Lago Limo or Col Bechei.

3. Sennes Plateau Traverse (Strenuous)

- Route: From Pederü to Rifugio Sennes, Rifugio Biella, and Lago di Braies.
- The distance between points is approximately 18 kilometers.
- Time: 7–8 hours
- Highlights: Alpine isolation, panoramic views, hut-to-lake finale.

For trekkers looking for a full-day adventure via diverse terrain. Begin with a climb to Rifugio Sennes, then proceed across the high plateau to Rifugio Biella. The descent into Lago di Braies is steep but spectacular, culminating in a refreshing foot soak and well-deserved supper.

It is also possible to reverse the path. Popular among Alta Via 1 hikers.

4. Fanes Circuit via Ju de Limo (moderate to strenuous)

- Route: Fanes Huts, Ju de Limo, Lago Limo, Gran Fanes, Capanna Alpina.

- Distance: Approximately 15 kilometers.
- Time: 6–7 hours
- Landscape: plateau, rolling alpine landscape, and woodland descent

A whole circle that encompasses all Fanes stands for: open sky, pristine lakes, limestone towers, and vast isolation. The path connects Alta Badia with Val di Fanes and is suited for point-to-point hiking with a return shuttle or taxi.

Difficulty Levels

- Beginner-Friendly: Braies Lake Loop, short walks from Capanna Alpina, or hikes with hut access from Pederü.
- Moderate Treks: Day hikes into the Fanes and Sennes plateaus, with clean routes and moderate climbs
- Strenuous options include cross-plateau climbs, hut-to-hut traverses, and expansions into the Lagazuoi and Tofane groups.

The elevation ranges from ~1,400m (Pederü) to ~2,500m (plateau peak). The weather can change quickly, so dress in layers and get an early start.

Highlights and Moments

- Lago di Braies before dawn: unparalleled stillness and meditation.
- Sunrises on Fanes Plateau: Gentle colors wash across open stone.
- Rifugio Lavarella serves Ladin food, including speck dumplings and house-made elderflower syrup.
- Alpine animal sightings include marmots, ibex, and uncommon eagles.
- Lago Limo: Remote, glacial, and quiet—soul-calming tranquility.

Access and Logistics

Main Gateways:

- San Vigilio di Marebbe provides access to Pederü, Fanes, and Sennes.
- Braies (Pragser Tal) - for Rifugio Biella and the lake of Braies
- La Villa/Badia/Capanna Alpina - Alta Badia side of the park.

Public transportation:

- Summer buses depart from Dobbiaco, Brunico, Cortina, and Alta Badia.

- Shuttles to Pederü and Lago di Braies are essential during peak season.

Best months:

- Late June until mid-October.
- Wildflowers peak in July.
- September delivers larch colors and peaceful trails.

Recommended Rifugi

- Rifugio Fanes is charming, renowned, and family-run. Known for its friendly and story-filled welcome.
- Rifugio Lavarella: Close to Fanes, with craft beer brewed on-site and delicious food.
- Rifugio Sennes is remote, sunny, and panoramic. Ideal for extended visits.
- Rifugio Biella (Seekofel Hütte) is sparse and located high above the Lago di Braies. Full of personality.

Book in advance, especially from mid-July to August.

Insider Tips

- Stay the night: Fanes is not a day-trip destination. Stay overnight at Fanes or Lavarella to experience the mellow beauty of this region.

- Legends exist here: Discover Ladin myths about princesses transformed into marmots, mountains made of stone tears, and hidden kingdoms beneath the peaks.
- Bring binoculars: Wildlife is abundant, and early mornings are ideal for seeing chamois and eagles.
- Quiet season: Early October brings bright light, golden larches, and an almost empty park—just be prepared for early snow.

Lago di Braies and Extension Hikes

Lago di Braies is sometimes introduced with a photograph of mirror-clear water reflecting a wooden boathouse, with Croda del Becco rising like a cathedral behind it. It's beautiful. Unreal, even. Nonetheless, the photograph barely scratched the surface. Because, while most visitors stop at the seashore, the real enchantment occurs when you go past the camera frame and continue on.

This is not just a lake. It is the northern entrance of Fanes-Sennes-Braies Nature Park. It is a trailhead. A point of departure. A point at which the landscape transitions into a trip.

Why is Lago di Braies important?

Yes, this is one of Europe's most photographed lakes. And, yes, during peak season, you will have a regular stream of admirers. But Braies is much more than its fame.

- It marks the commencement of the Alta Via 1, one of the Dolomites' most famous long-distance paths.
- It serves as a launching platform for high alpine terrain that most day-trippers cannot access.
- It's both accessible and remote at the same time—easy to get to, yet immediately expansive once you lace up and move forward.

- It is linked to Ladin mythology, WWII history, and geological wonder.

Stay an hour or a week. Braies is stunning in either case. But go into its folds and it shows itself.

Lago di Braies: The Classic Loop

1. Lakeside Circuit (Easy)

- Route: A round walk around the lake.
- Distance: 3.6 kilometers.
- Duration: 1–1.5 hours
- Elevation: low, with a few stairs and rocky parts on the far side.

The lake's loop trek is one of the Dolomites' most accessible and satisfying short hikes. Begin from the boathouse and follow the path clockwise for the best light and fewer tourists early on.

The western shore is smooth and wide. The eastern side climbs through the forest, skirting cliffs and providing framed lake views through pine boughs. Benches appear only when needed. Every step is accompanied by birdsong and the calm lap of water.

Best in the early morning, before the light rises and the silence fades.

Extension Hikes Beyond the Lake

2. To Rifugio Biella via Forcella Sora Forno (moderate to strenuous)

- Route: Lago di Braies, path 1 - Forcella Sora Forno - Rifugio Biella
- Distance: around 7.5 km one way.
- Time: 3.5 to 4.5 hours
- Elevation gain: approximately 900 m.

This is where Alta Via 1 begins and where the throngs disperse.

The walk ascends steeply along track 1 into the stone folds behind Croda del Becco (Seekofel). The vegetation thins as views open—first to the lake far below, then to the stark limestone saddle of Forcella Sora Forno, a 2,389-meter wind-whipped mountain pass.

Beyond, Rifugio Biella (Seekofel Hütte) rests like a ship on a stone sea: simple, exposed, and unforgettable. Continue for multi-day climbs, or relax with mountain tea and sweeping silence, which few expect so close to a hotspot.

3. To Fojedora Alm and Malga Foresta (moderate, peaceful)

- Braies Lake - Trail 19 or 20 - Valle di Foresta.
- Distance: approximately 10 kilometers round trip.
- Time: 3–4 hours
- Terrain: Gentle forest and open pastures.

If you want to be calm without ascending, this is the way to go. The walk leads into the Val di Foresta, a deep, wooded valley that rarely appears in flashy tourism brochures. Meadows lead onto grazing country, with wooden fences and wildflowers spread like confetti.

Malga Foresta, a classic mountain chalet, offers speck platters and homemade Kaiserschmarrn. Far from the cameras, Braies begins to breathe again.

4. Rifugio Vallandro via Sennes Plateau (strenuous)

- Rifugio Biella - Trail 6 - Rifugio Sennes - Rifugio Vallandro
- Distance: around 16 km one way.
- Time: 6–7 hours
- Elevation gain: approximately 1,200 m.

A true traverse for experienced hikers. From the lake to Rifugio Biella, travel via the Sennes Plateau, a large open expanse with few trees and views that stretch to infinity. Descend to Rifugio Vallandro (Plätzwiese), a lovely meadow with horses grazing and rugged peaks reaching the clouds.

This climb is frequently completed as part of a longer Alta Via 1 route, but it also stands alone as a powerful day (or overnight) trek.

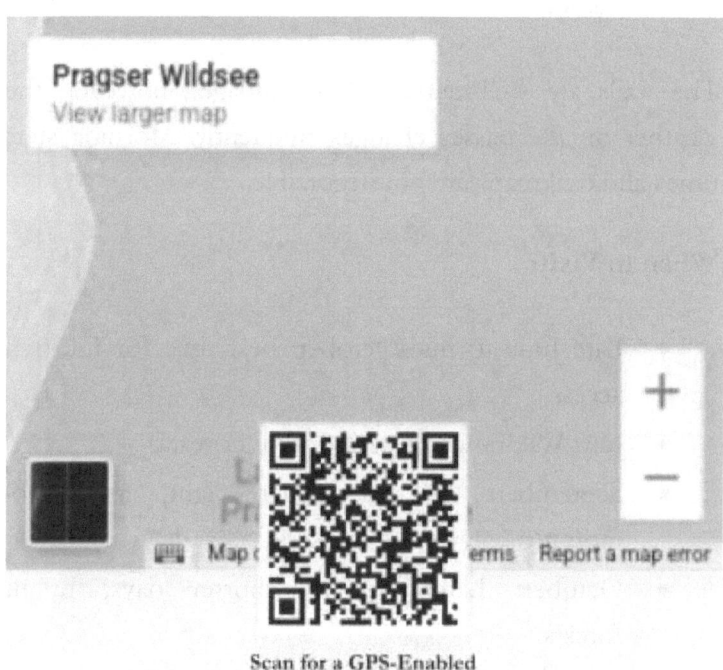

Scan for a GPS-Enabled Map Experience

Difficulty and Trail Conditions

- Beginner: The lake loop is approachable, especially for youngsters.
- Moderate: Hikes into Val di Foresta or toward Malga Foresta are relaxing and charming, with no technical challenges.
- Strenuous: High climbs to Rifugio Biella, Sennes, or Vallandro require stamina, decent boots, and alpine layering.

The trails are well-marked (CAI signage), however, the weather on the passes changes frequently. Morning start times and trail maps are not negotiable.

When to Visit?

- Late June to mid-October: best time for full trail access.
- July: Wildflower peak in Val di Foresta.
- September: quieter, golden light, and cool mornings.
- October: Larch season—shorter days, bright forests.

If possible, avoid the peak lake hours (10:30 am-3:30 pm) in July and August.

Access and Logistics

Nearest town: Braies (Pragser Tal)

Getting There:

- By car: Parking is accessible but restricted; arrive before 8 a.m. in summer.
- Public transportation: Shuttle buses from Dobbiaco, Villabassa, and Valdaora are mandatory from July to mid-September.

Lago di Braies access control: During high season, access is regulated.

- Reserve your parking or transportation spot in advance.
- Walking and biking is always allowed.

Rifugi:

- Rifugio Biella: Spartan yet magnificent; open June to September.
- Rifugio Sennes & Vallandro: Comfort-focused, open mid-June till early October.
- Malga Foresta: Day stop only—delicious and rustic, no overnight

Insider Tips

- Visit at dawn or dusk to experience the quiet, reflective lake and early light.
- Avoid weekends during high season; instead, visit midweek or in September.
- Stay nearby: at a guesthouse in Braies or Villabassa, or reserve Rifugio Biella for a rocky mountain getaway.
- Combine lake and plateau: Don't just take a photo. Make the lake the beginning, not the conclusion.

Tofane Group (Cortina d'Ampezzo Area)

Some mountain groups allow you in gently. The Tofane do not. They rise like a vertical wall over Cortina d'Ampezzo, a trio of cliffs and ridgelines that dominate the skyline and defy you to look away. This is where the Dolomites show off their muscle. Sheer, angular, and imposing—but also brimming with history, hidden paths, and some of the best scenic routes in the area.

Scan for a GPS-Enabled Map Experience

The Tofane Group is untamed and rough. Its peaks reach over 3,200 meters, its slopes still bear the scars of World

War I, and its routes range from family-friendly vistas to knife-edge via ferrata. But for those that trek it properly—on foot, with time, and with breath—it becomes much more than a backdrop. It becomes a story about stone, quiet, and magnitude.

Why Tofane Are Essential

- Visual Dominance: Easily the most imposing presence on Cortina.
- Dramatic geology includes steep cliffs, scree slopes, hanging ledges, and hidden plateaus.
- Historical Depth: World War I trenches, tunnels, and open-air battlefields
- Panoramic glory: 360-degree views from ridgelines and summits
- Trails range from small day walks to multi-day hut-to-hut traverses.

This is where hiking turns into high alpine immersion. It is not for the casual stroller, but it provides significant rewards.

Where It Is and What It Includes

The Tofane massif is located just northwest of Cortina d'Ampezzo in the Ampezzo Dolomites, which are part of the Parco Naturale delle Dolomiti d'Ampezzo. The group is anchored by three major peaks:

- Tofana di Mezzo (3,244 m)—the highest and most accessible
- Tofana di Dentro (3,238 m)—slightly more distant
- Tofana di Rozes (3,225 m) - most visually iconic, frequently photographed with its broad, curved south face.

This tight massif is the upper spine of the Dolomiti d'Ampezzo Nature Park, a protected area with tremendous biodiversity, high plateaus, and stunning alpine splendor.

Best Hiking Routes in the Tofane Group

1. Rifugio Dibona to Rifugio Giussani (Moderate)

- Route: Dibona-Valon de Tofana-Giussani.
- Distance: approximately 8 kilometers round trip.
- Time: 3–4 hours
- Elevation gain: approximately 500 m.

A strong introduction to Tofane's higher realm. The trek leads from Rifugio Dibona (which is accessible by car) to the amphitheatre beneath Tofana di Rozes. The majestic walls press in, and scree slopes ripple across the valley floor.

The final ascent to Rifugio Giussani, nestled in a saddle at 2,580 metres, feels unearthly.

Stay for lunch or prolong your day by ascending Forcella Fontananegra for breathtaking views of the Cinque Torri area.

2. Tofana di Rozes Circuit (Strenuous and Panoramic)

- Route: Rifugio Dibona, Giussani, Forcella Col dei Bos, and return by the lower trail.
- Distance: around 12-14 kilometers.
- Time: 6–7 hours
- Ideal for fit hikers seeking a wild circle around the most prominent Tofana summit.

This trip circles Tofana di Rozes, giving dramatic changes in scenery—from small scree routes to open alpine pastures to forested descents. One of the best all-day treks in the Cortina basin, but less well-known than the lake circuits and Tre Cime trails.

3. WWI Tunnel Route (Moderate and Historical)

- Route: Lagazuoi Cable Car, WWI Tunnel Path, Rifugio Dibona.
- Distance: around 10 kilometers.

- Time: 4–5 hours
- Highlights: Original war tunnels, observation posts, and mountain history

Although not formally part of the Tofane massif, they are connected by saddle routes and share the same geological basin. This climb descends from Rifugio Lagazuoi via tunnels and switchbacks created by WWI soldiers. It finally reaches the trail to Rifugio Dibona, which leads back to Cortina or farther into the Tofane group.

Bring a headlamp and be respectful; the route is both somber and dramatic.

4. Summit of Tofana di Mezzo (Strenuous/Lift-Assisted Option)

- Route: Top of Tofana cable car + Summit trail
- Distance: approximately 2-3 kilometers.
- Time: 1.5 to 2.5 hours.
- Elevation gain: ~200-300 meters.

Take the Freccia nel Cielo cable car from Cortina to the top station at Ra Valles, then follow a steep ridge walk to the summit of Tofana di Mezzo, the Dolomites' third-highest peak.

On a clear day, the vista extends from the Austrian Alps to the Brenta Group and beyond. Not recommended in inclement weather or without proper mountain footing. It's an absolute requirement for experienced hikers.

Difficulty Levels

- Moderate: Rifugio walks from Dibona to Giussani, WWI path descents, and plateau loops.
- Strenuous: Full-day circuits, summit walks, and anything with scree traverses or exposed ledges.
- Technical: Several via ferrata routes in the Tofane for those with equipment and climbing confidence (not covered here, but worth exploring).

This is true alpine hiking: exposed, steep, and challenging. Conditions change rapidly. Boots, poles, layers, and weather knowledge are necessary.

Best time to visit

- Late June to late September: Full trail and rifugio access.
- July and August: Rifugi open, longest daylight and busiest weeks.
- September is cooler and quieter, making it excellent for long-distance photography and clarity.

- Early October: Risk of early snow over 2,500 metres; check conditions.

Access and Logistics

Base: Cortina d'Ampezzo, the main hub for Tofane hikes.

- Excellent lodging range, transit alternatives, and gear shops.
- Buses to Passo Falzarego, Rifugio Dibona junction, and the cable car base

Cable Cars:

- Freccia nel Cielo: Tofana di Mezzo (closed during the off-season)
- Lagazuoi cable car provides access to the WWI crest and via ferrata trails.

Rifugi:

- Rifugio Dibona: The main trailhead hut, ideal for starting or concluding long days.
- Rifugio Giussani: Remote and authentic; overnight stay is recommended.
- Rifugio Lagazuoi: Ideal for connecting WWI hikes with panoramic pauses.

Highlights & Viewpoints

- Sunset at Tofana di Rozes: The rock sparkles with fire, best seen from Rifugio Scoiattoli or Passo Falzarego.
- Summit panoramas: From Tofana di Mezzo, it's an alpine dome with 360° peaks.
- WWI remnants: Look for artillery caves, observation slits, and collapsing bunkers built onto the cliffs.
- Forcella Fontananegra: A rugged, windy pass with views directly into the center of the Ampezzo basin.

Insider Tips

- Avoid midday starts: These hikes are high and exposed; early morning is safer and quieter.
- Bring a headlamp: Even non-tunnel pathways may travel through gloomy battle relics.
- Stay overnight in Giussani: the stars feel close enough to touch.
- Connect with other groups: The Tofane easily connects with Lagazuoi, Cinque Torri, and Fanes.

Conclusion

This isn't a gentle hike. This is full-height hiking—both physically and emotionally. There's something huge about walking here. Something that alters your perception of scale. The Tofane don't ask for attention; they accept it. In their shadows, you feel little. You also feel alive.

And when the wind blows across the high saddles, brushing against stone that has been remembered for ages, it feels like you're standing on the brink of something much larger than a mountain or map. It's like being in the Dolomites as they were meant to be felt: wild, enormous, and completely unforgettable.

Monte Pelmo and Civetta (Dolomiti Bellunesi)

In the gloomy southern reaches of the Dolomites, where crowds thin and mountains speak in lengthier sentences, two names stand out: Monte Pelmo and Monte Civetta.

They aren't the most trafficked. Not the most photographed. But for those who have walked beneath them, they are unforgettable. These are the Belluno Dolomites' giants, eerie in scale, stubborn in shape, and shrouded in a hush that is rare among the more famed northern massifs.

Civetta is known as the "wall of walls," a vertical stronghold that is five kilometers broad. Pelmo, on the other hand, stands alone like a throne—massive, compact, and solemn—hence the name "El Caregon del Padreterno" (God's Armchair). Between them are wild valleys, hanging lakes, WWI paths, and some of the best hut-to-hut terrain in the Dolomites.

Here is where loneliness returns. And where the Dolomites seem free again.

Why hike here?

- Monumental geology: towering cliffs, exposed plateaus, and vast rock amphitheaters

- Less congested trails: Even in summer, peaceful ridges and empty passes.
- Raw wilderness: Part of the Dolomiti Bellunesi National Park, one of the least developed regions in the Dolomites.
- World War I history: trenches, mule tracks, and fortifications along the ridges
- Diverse hiking: From gentle lakeside loops to strenuous alpine traverses.

Whether day hiking around Pelmo or circling Civetta on a multi-day route, this is a landscape that inspires awe rather than noise.

Where It is

This region is located in Veneto's Belluno province and forms the southern border of the Dolomites proper. The Civetta Group towers above Alleghe and Val di Zoldo, and Monte Pelmo is located just east of the Cortina-Alleghe-Zoldo triangle.

Compared to Cortina or Val Gardena, the towns here are quieter, the pace slower, and the trails wilder.

Top Hiking Routes around Monte Pelmo and Civetta

1. Monte Pelmo Circuit: Moderate to Strenuous

- Route: Passo Staulanza, Rifugio Venezia, Forcella d'Arcia, loop around Pelmo.
- Distance: approximately 13.5 km.
- Time: 6–7 hours
- Elevation gain: approximately 850 m.

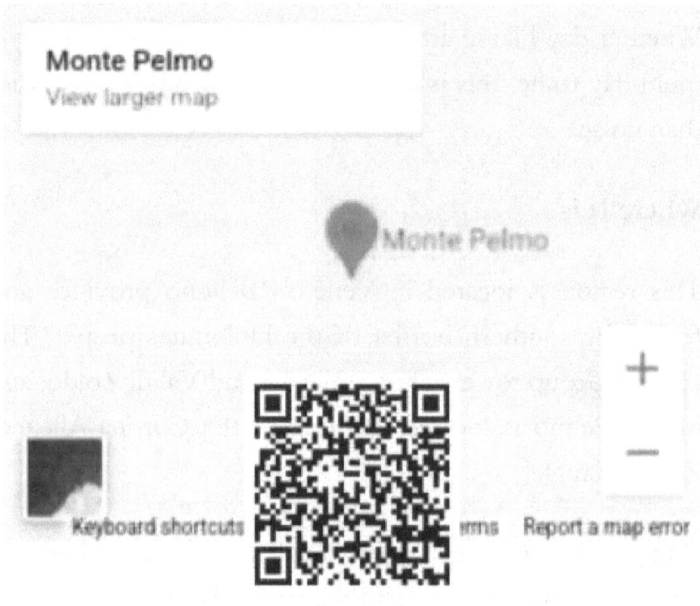

Scan for a GPS-Enabled Map Experience

This loop encircles Monte Pelmo, revealing its imposing mass from all sides. The trail ascends from Passo Staulanza through pine forests, past the grassy terraces of Rifugio Venezia, and then sharply into the high notch of Forcella d'Arcia (2,476 m).

The northern side features harsh terrain, including scree slopes, stone ledges, and long traverses. But the visual payoff is enormous—the north face of Pelmo, towering and glacial, framed by complete silence. Suitable for experienced hikers used to rugged alpine trails.

2. Civetta Loop via Alta Via 1 Segment (Strenuous, Multi-Day)

- Route: Alleghe – Rifugio Coldai – Rifugio Tissi – Val Civetta – return
- Distance: ~25–30 km total (2–3 days recommended)
- Elevation Gain: ~1,500–1,800 m total
- Highlights: Lake Coldai, Civetta's north wall, rifugio-to-rifugio immersion

Start from Alleghe or Palafavera, ascend through spruce forest to the high alpine basin of Lago Coldai, and spend the night at Rifugio Tissi, perched on a high shoulder facing Civetta's legendary wall.

By day two, descend into the Val Civetta basin, traversing below the cliffs along the Alta Via 1, and exit via Val Corpassa. Option to extend to Rifugio Vazzoler or Capanna Trieste. This is true alpine theater—colossal, rugged, unforgettable.

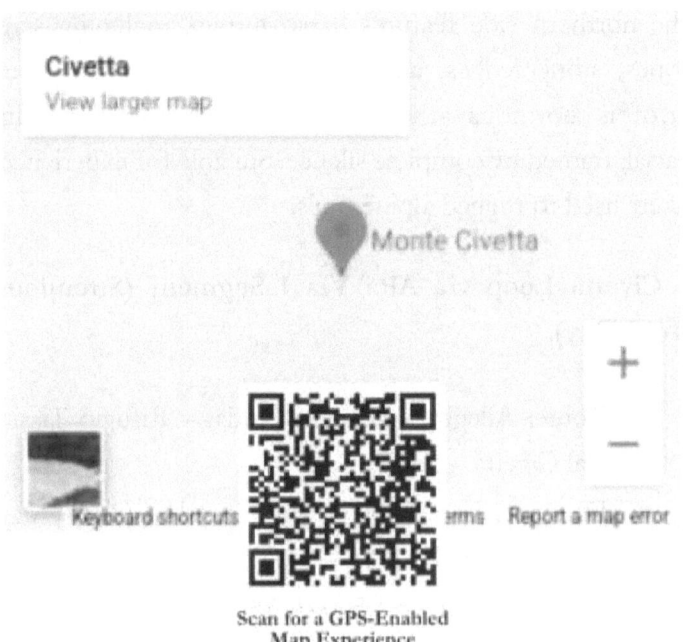

Scan for a GPS-Enabled Map Experience

3. Lake Coldai Day Hike (Moderate)

- Route: Palafavera – Rifugio Coldai – Lago Coldai
- Distance: approximately 9 kilometers round trip.

- Time: 4–5 hours
- Elevation gain: ~600 meters

A perfect day hike for those not ready for hut-to-hut journeys. The trail climbs steadily past malga pastures, enters larch forest, and opens suddenly to the glacial cirque of Lago Coldai, beneath the dramatic west face of Civetta.

Best in the morning, when reflections still dance across the water.

4. Dinosaur Footprints Trail (Easy to Moderate)

- Route: Passo Staulanza – Pelmo's western flank – Dinosaur track site
- Distance: ~5.5 km round trip
- Duration: 2-3 hours.
- Unique feature: Actual dinosaur footprints embedded in limestone

Yes—real dinosaur tracks. Left in soft mud 220 million years ago, fossilized, and now perched at 2,000 meters on a high Dolomite slope. It's a short hike, part forest, part scree slope, ending at a stone slab that once formed part of an ancient tidal flat. Especially rewarding for families and amateur geologists.

Difficulty Levels

- Easy: Lake Coldai, Dinosaur Trail
- Moderate: Monte Pelmo lower loops, day hikes to rifugi
- Strenuous: Full Pelmo circuit, Civetta traverse, AV1 segments
- Technical (Optional): Via Ferrata degli Alleghesi (Civetta summit)—not included here, but famed among climbers.

Trails are well-marked, but rocky and isolated. Weather moves quickly at 2,000+ meters. Early starts, good footwear, and layering are essential.

Best time to visit

- Late June to late September
- July: Wildflowers in the meadows, clear high passes
- August: Busiest around Alleghe and Coldai hut—book early
- September: Calm, golden larches, and quiet rifugi
- Early October: Possible, but early snow may close high routes.

Access and Logistics

Main Bases:

- Alleghe – for Civetta treks
- Selva di Cadore / Zoldo Alto – for Monte Pelmo access
- Passo Staulanza – trailhead for Pelmo circuit and the Dinosaur Trail

Public Transport: Regional buses from Belluno, Calalzo, or Cortina to Alleghe and Zoldo

Car Access: Recommended for flexibility; trailheads are often remote

Rifugi:

- Rifugio Venezia – classic mountain hut below Pelmo, welcoming and remote
- Rifugio Coldai – lakeside location with quick access from Palafavera
- Rifugio Tissi – perched high with Civetta's wall straight ahead
- Rifugio Vazzoler – quiet forest hut at the edge of Val Corpassa

Highlights & Viewpoints

- Sunrise from Rifugio Tissi: Light crawling down Civetta's wall—worth every ounce of ascent

- Lago Coldai reflections: Absolute alpine calm in early hours
- Monte Pelmo's north face: Glacial, silent, and overwhelming in scale
- Dinosaur slab on Pelmo: Time, frozen in rock
- Wild solitude: On Pelmo's backside or Civetta's flanks, one can go hours without seeing a soul

Insider Tips

- Book Tissi early: It's a favorite for Alta Via 1 hikers and sells out fast
- Early start for Pelmo circuit: Sun-exposed sections get hot and dry mid-day
- Avoid Civetta wall descent in fog or rain: The terrain is loose, and visibility drops fast.
- Bring binoculars: Ibex and chamois are common on Civetta's ledges.
- Combine with AV1: Both Pelmo and Civetta appear early on the Alta Via 1—worth merging for multi-day hikes.

Conclusion

Some peaks shout. These two speak slowly. But the message lingers.

Monte Pelmo stands alone—massive, self-contained, eternal. It doesn't compete. It simply is. Civetta is different. It confronts, dares, overwhelms. You go beneath it, and something shifts. Something real.

In these southern Dolomites, there's space again. Fewer people. Bigger skies. Longer silences. And in that calm, you receive the rarest thing of all—a Dolomite experience that's totally your own.

Local Culture along the Trails

Walking through the Dolomites is never solely about the scenery. It is also about discovering the distinct blend of people, traditions, flavors, and stories forged by centuries spent in the highlands. These valleys are reverberating with many languages, cultures, and culinary delights, all flawlessly woven into the fabric of the routes.

Embracing this local culture entails enjoying fresh mountain cheese at a little malga, relishing slow-smoked speck after a tough hike, or hearing Ladin legends whispered via the wind and woven into the settlements itself.

Hiking here without learning about the local culture is like missing half of the experience.

Ladin Heritage and Villages

Timeless Voices Among Peaks

Hidden among the central valleys of the Dolomites, the Ladin people preserve a culture older than Italy itself. Ladin is more than just a language; it is the core of a proud, tenacious community that has deep roots in the mountain valleys of Alta Badia, Val Gardena, Val di Fassa, and Ampezzo.

Villages to Discover:

- Ortisei (Urtijëi) is a thriving artistic community in Val Gardena, notable for its woodcarving workshops. Handcrafted wooden sculptures are created here by artists, following a tradition passed down through centuries.
- San Cassiano: In Alta Badia, this community ideally combines history and luxury. The Ursus Ladinicus

- museum displays ancient antiquities and graphically depicted local stories.
- Colfosco and Corvara: Nestled behind stunning cliffs, these settlements provide glimpses into traditional Ladin farm life and architecture, with wooden balconies draped in flowering geraniums and painted frescoes on small chapels.
- Vigo di Fassa (Vich) is the Rosengarten group's gateway, and its museum, Ladin de Fascia, beautifully depicts the profound ties between Ladin culture and mountain nature.

Walking through these communities is like feeling history beneath your feet, with each small street, wooden chalet, and tiny church whispering stories older than recorded memory.

Alpine Cuisine to Savor Following the Hike

A beautiful day trekking in the Dolomites does not end at the trail's edge, but at the table. Alpine cuisine is more than simply food; it's a celebration of local ingredients, traditions, and changing seasons.

Iconic Foods You Must Try:

- Speck Alto Adige is a cured ham seasoned with juniper, salt, and pepper that is slowly smoked over

beechwood. This delicacy tastes best when thinly sliced and served with freshly made rye bread with mountain cheese.
- Knödel (Canederli) are hearty dumplings cooked from bread soaked in milk, eggs, smoked speck, or mountain cheese, seasoned with herbs, and gently boiled. Serve them in a warm broth or with melted butter and grated Parmesan.
- Kaiserschmarrn: Golden, fluffy shredded pancakes topped with powdered sugar and served with handmade berry compote. After hours of difficult paths, a warm and pleasant ending.
- Schlutzkrapfen are half-moon-shaped pasta filled with spinach and fresh ricotta, served with melted butter, parmesan, and crispy sage leaves—a simple but delicious traditional.

Every community, rifugio, or family-run restaurant serves variations on local cuisine passed down through generations. Tasting these foods is tasting history.

Alpine Dairies (Malgas) and Cheese Tasting

Flavors Developed from Mountain Meadows

As pathways snake through high-altitude pastures, the mellow ringing of cowbells serves as a soothing reminder that dairy farming has sculpted these mountains for millennia. Malgas, or small, seasonal alpine dairies, dot the hillsides, their rustic wooden facilities fitting perfectly with the natural surroundings.

Why stop at Malga?

- Fresh, Artisan Cheese: Local cheesemakers manufacture their dairy products with age-old traditions, fresh alpine milk, and natural pasturage rich in wildflowers and herbs, resulting in distinct flavors that cannot be replicated anywhere.
- Authentic Tastings: Malga visits are more than just transactions. Cheesemakers proudly serve tastings of their fresh ricotta, powerful aged cheeses, creamy formaggio di malga, and sour yogurt, as well as handcrafted preserves and fresh bread.
- Warm Hospitality: Pausing at a malga seems like entering a simpler, slower world. Visitors are cordially welcomed by the hosts, who are eager to share stories about mountain life, customs, and handicrafts.

Favorite Malaga to visit:

- Malga Geisler (Val di Funes): Located beneath the spectacular Odle peaks, this establishment is famed for its outstanding cheeses and panoramic dining.

- Malga Foresta (Lago di Braies area): A welcoming and rustic spot to relax, eat local cheese plates, and sip elderflower cordial.
- Malga Contrin (Val di Fassa): Enjoy fresh cheeses combined with locally brewed beer.

Visiting these alpine dairies brings the traveler closer to the source, allowing them to taste the landscape in each meal.

Local Legends and WWI Remnants

The Dolomites contain stories inside their stone. Legends and histories are engraved into these mountains, passed down via generations of storytellers and reinforced by actual remnants scattered along the pathways.

Legends from Ladin Culture

- The towering Rosengarten peaks glow pink at sunset, according to locals, and are said to be King Laurin's famous rose garden, which was enchanted so that no one could see it until dusk.
- Fanes Kingdom (Fanes-Sennes-Braies): According to Ladin mythology, a flourishing kingdom hidden deep within these plateaus was controlled by warrior queens and mountain spirits who fiercely protected their territory.

Listening to these narratives while walking these landscapes transforms a stroll into a lyrical pilgrimage—a journey through layers of myth and magic.

Remains of World War I

The serene mountains of today were not always so tranquil. The Dolomites' pathways are imprinted with the legacy of World War I, when Italian and Austrian soldiers fought hard engagements on tough, hilly terrain.

- Lagazuoi Tunnels: Near Cortina d'Ampezzo, tunnels built directly into the mountain provide spooky pathways that were formerly utilized as military shelters and supply routes. Hikers today walk through history, a depressing yet intriguing journey.
- Cinque Torri Open-Air Museum has accessible pathways that weave through painstakingly recreated trenches, observation points, and defenses. Informative signs tell moving human stories of courage and survival.
- Monte Piano (Misurina): Trenches, barbed wire, bunkers, and shell craters have been conserved as a historical site—moving and intensely emotive, they provide a glimpse into a sad past.

Seeing these historical remnants directly lends tremendous meaning to your footsteps, bringing a human dimension to natural beauty.

Why should you embrace local culture?

To properly experience the Dolomites, one must embrace more than just the paths and scenery. This means:

- Savoring meals that reflect centuries-old traditions, prepared with ingredients grown in the regions you've traversed.
- Pausing at mountain dairies to sample cheese flavored by alpine pastures, made by families with a long history of land ownership.
- Wandering through communities where Ladin culture lives, hearing ancient languages spoken proudly, and gently stepping into the mountains' living past.
- Reflecting calmly along historical roads, contemplating the strength and tragedy contained in these tranquil places.

Embracing local culture on the trails enriches each step. It elevates trekking from a basic physical challenge to meaningful travel, and gorgeous excursions into lasting personal ties. The Dolomites become more than just stunning scenery; they are very human environments, full of tradition, community, resilience, and memory.

The ultimate joy of experiencing these mountains is that they unveil their secrets slowly and gently, inviting each tourist into their unfolding story.

Practical Tips and Advice

What Every Hiker Should Know Before Getting On the Trail

The nuances nearly always make the difference between a decent hiking vacation and a terrific one, regardless of how gorgeous the peaks or thrilling the paths are. Planning is not about overscheduling; rather, it is about awareness, confidence, and rhythm. Getting to the trailhead smoothly, carrying what's important, avoiding the noon throngs, ordering a meal in Ladin or German without fumbling—

these are the moments that make the journey feel effortless, rooted, and satisfying.

Whether you're trekking past Rifugi for three days or crossing the Dolomites on Alta Via routes for two weeks, there are a few things you should know to save time, money, worry, and sometimes even more.

Trail Safety and Essentials

Although not as harsh as the Himalayas or the Patagonian Andes, the Dolomites are alpine. This means that the weather changes quickly, the landscape varies greatly, and even experienced hikers can be surprised by the elevation climb.

Safety fundamentals:

- Start early: Thunderstorms are prevalent in the afternoons during the summer. Begin hiking by 8:00 a.m., particularly for high passes.
- Know your trail: Study route profiles rather than just distance. A 10-kilometer track with 1,000 meters of elevation gain differs from a flat valley hike.
- Layer wisely: morning chill, midday sun, and unexpected rain. Breathable base layers, a strong

midlayer, and a waterproof shell are absolute must-haves.
- Poles are especially useful on scree descents, snowfields, and knee-saving switchbacks.
- Navigation is important: Although routes are well-marked, fog and snowfields can confuse. Download offline maps (e.g., Komoot, Gaia GPS) and save a paper map for safety.
- Emergency numbers: In Italy, dial 112 for mountain rescue. Mountain lodges and localized apps frequently list local services.

Essentials to Carry:

- Minimum of 2L of water (with purification tabs or filter if planning longer travels).
- Protein and salt-rich snacks include cheese, almonds, cured meat, and dried fruit.
- Compact headlight (storms or delays occur).
- First aid kit: blister treatment, antihistamines, and bandage wrap.
- Sun protection: high SPF, sunglasses, and a hat.
- Lightweight emergency bivvy or heat blanket.

Know your limitations. In the Dolomites, going back is prudent, not weak. The mountain will be there tomorrow.

Trailhead Parking and Regulations

Some trailheads are wonderfully remote. Others are well-known, crowded, and carefully regulated, particularly during the summer. Knowing which is which makes a huge impact.

General Rules:

- The majority of trailhead parking is paid, so bring coins or credit cards. The fees range from €6 to €20 per day, depending on location.
- Summer shuttles: From June to September, places including Tre Cime, Lago di Braies, and Seiser Alm offer shuttle services.
- Reservation-only zones: Lago di Braies and Tre Cime parking frequently require online reservations. Without it, you will be denied entry.
- Parking spots near popular huts and lakes can fill up quickly, especially in August, as early as 7:30 a.m.

Parking Smarter:

- Use satellite villages: Stay at Dobbiaco instead of Braies, or La Villa instead of Passo Gardena, and then shuttle in.
- Take lifts up and trek down, particularly around Seceda and Rosetta Plateau. Reduces traffic and introduces new perspectives.

- Stay overnight near the trailhead: To avoid day-trippers, start early from a nearby cabin or agriturismo.

The signage is good. However, don't assume legality. Cars parked outside zones, on grass, or in restricted areas are punished.

Crowds and How to Avoid Them

Yes, the Dolomites have achieved Instagram stardom. And yes, there are congestion in the summer. But the crowd map is predictable and manageable.

Where Crowds Are:

- Tre Cime loop (July/August mid-morning to late afternoon).
- Lago di Braies (from sunrise until early sunset).
- Seceda ridgeline (particularly from the first lift up)
- Alpe di Siusi (day-tripper hotspot during peak season)

How to outspace the crowd:

- Sleep above the masses: Stay in rifugi like Locatellilike as Locatelli or Fanes and watch the people disperse around 4 p.m.

- Begin well before sunrise: It's more than just taking images. You will have entire valleys to yourself for hours.
- Visit during the ideal shoulder seasons: late June and mid-September. Most of the huts are still open. Trails are quieter.
- Aim for lesser-known trails, such as the ridge above Tre Cime. Hike Val di Funes instead of Alpe di Siusi. Walk to Lake Limedes instead of Braies.

Wilderness still exists in the Dolomites. You only have to get up early enough to meet it.

Travel Insurance

Mountain rescue in Italy isn't always free. A helicopter evacuation can cost thousands of dollars. Regular travel insurance may not always cover high-altitude hiking or via ferrata.

What to Look For:

- Rescue coverage includes helicopter evacuation and medical transport.
- Adventure sports clause: Unless clearly stated, some insurance exclude hiking beyond 2,000 metres or via ferrata.
- Trip interruptions include missed connections due to weather, hut closures, or injury.

- Gear covering is optional but useful for photographers and climbers with expensive equipment.

Providers to Explore:

- World Nomads
- Global Rescue
- Austrian Alpine Club (provides good rescue-only plans at a cheap annual charge).

Proof of coverage may be required at specific cabins or on via ferrata climbs.

Budgeting

The Dolomites provide a wide range of versatility. Spend like a mountaineer on a shoestring or like a bon vivant on a gourmet retreat. Most hikers fall somewhere in the middle.

Sample Budget (Daily Average):

- Rifugio overnight (half-board): €60 to €80.
- Trail lunch/snacks: €10 to €15.
- Lift pass (one-way): €15–€25.
- A multi-day lift card costs between €60 and €100 (Dolomiti Supersummer or Val Gardena passes).

- Bus/shuttle tickets cost €3-€10 per leg.

Ways to save:

- Bring a reusable water bottle to fill at mountain springs (safe and cold).
- Eat dinner in the rifugio and pack a lunch to leave.
- Choose lodges that provide CI/CAI membership discounts (Austrian Alpine Club also applies).
- Book multiple-night stays to get discounts.
- Do not skimp on experience. A beer at sunset on a rifugio patio is far more valuable than the price.

Language Tips for Hikers

The Dolomites are linguistically diverse; Italian, German, and Ladin are all widely spoken, frequently in the same village. English is frequently understood in tourist areas, but a little effort in the local language goes a long way.

Useful Phrases

Basic Greetings and Courtesies

Hello

- Italian: Ciao / Buongiorno
- German: Hallo / Guten Tag

- Ladin: Bun dé

Goodbye

- Italian: Arrivederci
- German: Auf Wiedersehen / Tschüss
- Ladin: A se vedëi

Good Evening

- Italian: Buonasera
- German: Guten Abend
- Ladin: Buna sëira

Good Night

- Italian: Buonanotte
- German: Gute Nacht
- Ladin: Buna nuet

Please

- Italian: Per favore
- German: Bitte
- Ladin: Per plasé

Thank you

- Italian: Grazie

- German: Danke
- Ladin: Grazia

You're welcome

- Italian: Prego
- German: Bitte schön
- Ladin: Da plasé

Useful Questions

Where is the trail?

- Italian: Dove si trova il sentiero?
- German: Wo ist der Wanderweg?
- Ladin: Ancue al troi?

How far is it?

- Italian: Quanto dista?
- German: Wie weit ist es?
- Ladin: Co l é luntan?

Is it difficult?

- Italian: È difficile?
- German: Ist es schwierig?
- Ladin: É dëra?

Where is the nearest hut/refuge?

- Italian: Dov'è il rifugio più vicino?
- German: Wo ist die nächste Hütte?
- Ladin: Ancue é l rifugio plu vëin?

What time does the lift open?

- Italian: A che ora apre la funivia?
- German: Wann öffnet die Seilbahn?
- Ladin: A che ora l è verta la funivia?

Accommodation & Food

Do you have a room?

- Italian: Avete una camera disponibile?
- German: Haben Sie ein freies Zimmer?
- Ladin: Vëives na stüa libra?

One night, please

- Italian: Una notte, per favore
- German: Eine Nacht, bitte
- Ladin: Na notë, per plasé

I have a reservation

- Italian: Ho una prenotazione

- German: Ich habe eine Reservierung
- Ladin: Ai na prenotaziun

Where is the dining room?

- Italian: Dov'è la sala da pranzo?
- German: Wo ist das Esszimmer?
- Ladin: Ancue é la stüa da mangé?

I'm vegetarian

- Italian: Sono vegetariano/a
- German: Ich bin Vegetarier/in
- Ladin: Sön vegetarian

Emergencies & Essentials

I need help

- Italian: Ho bisogno di aiuto
- German: Ich brauche Hilfe
- Ladin: Ai besögn d'ajüdë

Call the Rescue

- Italian: Chiama il soccorso
- German: Rufen Sie die Bergrettung
- Ladin: Ciamé l socors

I'm lost

- Italian: Mi sono perso/a
- German: Ich habe mich verirrt
- Ladin: Më soi pers

I'm injured

- Italian: Mi sono fatto/a male
- German: Ich habe mich verletzt
- Ladin: Më soi fat mal

What's the weather forecast?

- Italian: Qual è la previsione del tempo?
- German: Wie ist die Wettervorhersage?
- Ladin: Co é la previsiun dla orëa?

Practical Tips:

- Menus frequently blend languages. Don't be shocked to find "Schlutzkrapfen" listed under "Primi Piatti."
- Trail markers feature local names, such as Tre Cime (Drei Zinnen) and Seceda (Ladin).
- Staff at Rifugi appreciate simple greetings in the local tongue.

- Language represents connection. And connection is what makes a hike memorable.

Finally, hiking in the Dolomites is about more than just where your boots finish up. It's about how ready your mind and senses are to receive what the land has to offer. Knowing the regulations, customs, back doors, and quiet hours all make a difference.

It transforms the journey into a rhythm. The road toward something that flows effortlessly, meaningfully, and gracefully. The mountains remember this more than anything else.

Made in United States
Troutdale, OR
04/29/2025